10—

ADV 9853
u

Peter Matthiessen

Twayne's United States Authors Series

Frank Day, Editor

Clemson University

TUSAS 587

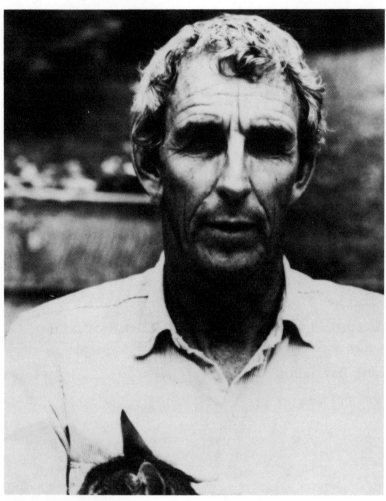

PETER MATTHIESSEN
© Rue Matthiessen.
Courtesy of Random House.

Peter Matthiessen

William Dowie

Southeastern Louisiana University

Twayne Publishers
A Division of G. K. Hall & Co. • Boston

Peter Matthiessen
William Dowie

Copyright 1991 by G. K. Hall & Co.
All rights reserved.
Published by Twayne Publishers
A division of G. K. Hall & Co.
70 Lincoln Street
Boston, Massachusetts 02111

Copyediting supervised by India Koopman.
Book production by Gabrielle B. McDonald.
Typeset in Garamond by Graphic Sciences Corporation, Cedar Rapids, Iowa.

First published 1991.
10 9 8 7 6 5 4 3 2 1

Library of Congress Cataloging-in-Publication Data

Dowie, William, 1940-
    Peter Matthiessen / William Dowie.
        p.   cm. — (Twayne's United States authors series ; TUSAS 587)
    Includes bibliographical references and index.
    ISBN 0-8057-7635-4
    1. Matthiessen, Peter—Criticism and interpretation.   I. Title.
    II. Series.
    PS3563.A8584Z64   1991
    813'.54—dc20   91-2967

For Alba,
the love of a lifetime,
at least

Contents

Preface

A book is a chain of events. This one began on 5 February 1988, the night I first heard Peter Matthiessen speak.

It had snowed heavily all that Friday afternoon, and by evening, with still no end in sight, the streets of Watertown, Massachusetts, were white and crunchy. Gripping the steering wheel tightly, I guided my Maxima along the twin furrows plowed by other cars, its windshield wipers batting furiously to keep up with the downfall. I had second thoughts about being out. Was a lecture by Matthiessen worth braving a storm for? Earlier in the day, it had seemed an excellent idea; for, at midpoint in my sabbatical, finished with one project and in search of another, I saw Matthiessen as a possible subject on the basis of what little I had read by him. Now, however, the weather loomed as an unfavorable auspice. Visibility was low and driving slow. There was no way I could make the 7:30 start. Backing the car alongside a sidewalk high with snowdrift, I consoled myself with the likelihood that the conditions would make for a small turnout and, consequently, a good chance of meeting the author afterwards.

As I climbed the wide, stately steps of the high-school auditorium and walked inside, I was astonished. The cavernous 900-capacity room showed only spots of empty seats. Matthiessen clearly had a following larger and more loyal than I had imagined.

When he arrived, also late because of the weather, he walked to the microphone, shed his sport jacket, raised it toward the audience and asked, "Has everybody seen my jacket?" He then draped it over the back of a chair, his debt to propriety apparently paid. Tall and craggily handsome, his face leathery from wind and sun, Matthiessen the man looked, despite his sixty-one years, every bit the adventurer of his famous expeditions to exotic locales. Matthiessen the lecturer—behind podium, microphone, and tie—resembled a captive lion, out of place but proud and capable of adaptation. He spoke easily about the course of his career, read from a recent story about the failure of American idealism, "Lumumba Lives," and finally answered questions frankly and attentively.

Everything about the evening encouraged me to look more deeply into Matthiessen's work: the haunting, portentous rhythm of the story, his personal candor, and the diversity and intensity of his appeal—the latter demonstrated by the varied constituencies represented in this snow-braving crowd. Some came to hear him talk about Zen (the following day he was to give an all-day workshop on Zen meditation); others had questions about ecology and wildlife; many were curious to see the traveler with whom they had vicariously trekked on expeditions around the world; and fiction lovers attended the lecture as devoutly as if Joseph Heller or John Hawkes were reading. The evening was impressive, but it didn't end as I had hoped. Matthiessen was so mobbed afterwards that I didn't even attempt meeting him then. Our meeting would come later.

Eventually Matthiessen did become the project of my remaining sabbatical and beyond. In writing about his books, my principal methodology has been simply to respond to the texts themselves. I purposely delayed studying the major reviews and the criticism (lean but vigorous) until after I had formed my own interpretations. In a real sense, the shape of my work was presaged by three facts that first evening: the diversity of Matthiessen's appeal, the superb artistry of the story he read, and his approachability.

Matthiessen's wide appeal derives from the varied nature of his work. I have therefore structured the book to emphasize the different functions he performs in his writing: novelist, naturalist, adventurer, explorer, advocate, and pilgrim. The only books of Matthiessen I do not treat are his children's book, *Seal Pool* (1972), his edition, with introduction, of George Catlin's *North American Indians* (1989), and *African Silences* (1991) which appeared after this book had been readied for publication. In each grouping of work, I try to sift the wheat from the chaff, although in the case of a writer as careful as Matthiessen, there isn't a lot of chaff.

Hearing him read from the searing "Lumumba Lives" was an omen that, although he has written more nonfiction than fiction, I would value the latter more highly. In a sense, Matthiessen's very appeal as a writer of nonfiction may have checked the ascent of his reputation as a novelist. Since many of his themes overlap in the two genres, readers reflexively lump the two together. Even an occasional critic misses the imaginative fire behind his novels because the settings and concerns are so similar to his nonfiction. Bruce Bawer's belittling "Nature Boy: the Novels of Peter Matthiessen," for example, reads Matthiessen's nonfiction and fiction together as a seamless indictment of Western civilization. I contend that when Matthiessen indicts, he does so specifically, never criticizing a notion as inclusive as Western civilization, in which he has a vested interest. Nor, in his fiction and nonfiction, is indictment the central thrust. The focus is both more positive and more varied, as indicated by the specifics of my chapters.

Matthiessen is moved in life and in writing by the contemplative urge, which—in its highest form—seeks unity with its beloved object. And nature is often the subject of his contemplation. His central insight is that in order to attain such union, man must experience himself as part of nature and realize that nature, even in its wildest heart, is part of him. Although this insight and other connections unify both Matthiessen's nonfiction and his fiction, my study argues that the fiction is of a higher order. Thematically and technically, his fiction goes further than his nonfiction. His best novels, in fact, have altered and expanded the genre.

Finally, my book has had the advantage of two extended conversations with Peter Matthiessen. He, indeed, has been an approachable subject, twice inviting me to lunch with himself and his wife, Maria, at their Sagaponack, New York, house. The visits occurred in winter (13 January 1989) and summer (10 August 1989). Matthiessen kindly answered all my questions in the midst of a busy writing schedule, during which he was working on his recently published *Killing Mister Watson*. I am also indebted to him for reading my manuscript and offering factual corrections, as well as for abstaining from matters of interpretation. Whatever errors remain, of course, are solely mine.

Acknowledgments

Thanks, first of all, to my editors Liz Fowler and Frank Day for their salient advice and encouragement. Also a part of the chain that became this book were Bill Parrill, who knows more contemporary fiction than anyone I know; Rob Taylor, who discovered Matthiessen for me; and James Salter, a writers' writer. I am particularly indebted to Southeastern Louisiana University and its then president, Larry Crain, for the sabbatical that allowed the project to begin.

Even further back along the chain was Edward J. Romagosa, S.J., my great teacher. More recently, Russ Pottle, Paul Montgomery, Mark Taylor, and Christine Taylor-McKenna contributed, each in a unique way. And most immediately, I am grateful to Joe Lane of the University of New Mexico Library and especially to Donna Jacques of the Brandeis University Library for their timely assistance. The thanks I owe to Peter Matthiessen are best expressed in my preface.

Chronology

1965   Trustee, New York Zoological Society (resigns 1978). *At Play in the Fields of the Lord* published (nominated for National Book Award).

1967   Grand Cayman turtle schooner voyage. Publishes *Oomingmak* and *Shorebirds*.

1968–1969   Conducts research in Delano, California.

1969–1970   Travels to Africa, Indian Ocean, Australia. *Sal Si Puedes* published. Begins study of Zen Buddhism.

1971   *Blue Meridian* published.

1972   Wife, Deborah, dies of cancer. *The Tree Where Man Was Born* published (nominated for National Book Award).

1973   Journeys on 250-mile trek across the Himalayas with zoologist George Schaller.

1974   Elected to National Institute of Arts and Letters.

1975   *Far Tortuga* published.

1975–1979   Travels and conducts research among American Indians; journeys to Africa, South America, Canada.

1978   Publishes *The Snow Leopard*.

1979   *The Snow Leopard* wins National Book Award. Matthiessen receives the Brandeis University Creative Arts Award.

1980   Marries Maria Eckhart.

1981   Becomes a Zen Monk.

1983   *In the Spirit of Crazy Horse* published.

1984   *Indian Country* published.

1985   Receives Gold Medal for Distinction in Natural History, the Academy of Natural Sciences, Philadelphia. Publishes *Nine-Headed Dragon River*.

1986   *Men's Lives* published.

1989   *On the River Styx and Other Stories* published. Teaches creative writing seminar at Yale.

1990   *Killing Mister Watson* published.

1991   *African Silences* published. *At Play in the Fields of the Lord* made into a film.

Chapter One

Bearings: New York, New Haven, Paris, Long Island, the World

If you're traveling from the north as I was that cold, blustery mid-January day, the way to Peter Matthiessen's home in Sagaponack, New York, is by ferry. The New London chugs out of the harbor past the U.S. naval docks, where a nuclear submarine sits, on into the expanse of water called Plum Gut—a wide pass between Fishers Island to the north, where Matthiessen used to summer with his family as a boy, and Long Island to the south, where he now lives. The ocean wind rips through Plum Gut, and the seas roll roughly enough to cause seasickness in landlubbers. On the port side in the distance lies the seagirt lighthouse called Race Rock, after which Matthiessen titled his first book.

The whole trip, by means of three separate ferries, becomes a kind of baptism, the initiate symbolically transported into the water world of Peter Matthiessen, whose recent *Killing Mister Watson* (1990) is set in the Ten Thousand Islands area of coastal Florida. Before that, there was *On the River Styx and Other Stories* (1989) and *Men's Lives* (1986), about the fishermen of Long Island's South Fork, among whose number Matthiessen once counted himself. Even the navy submarine in New London is emblematic, as Matthiessen joined the navy in World War II, was stationed at Pearl Harbor, and set his third novel, *Raditzer* (1961), on board a navy vessel.

The last in a chain of three ferries delivers visitor and car to Sag Harbor, a quiet onetime whaling village, whose lovely cemetery contains the Monument to Masters, a statue of whalers being tossed about on the high seas by an attacking whale. As it turns out, Matthiessen is descended on his father's side from a 17th-century whaling captain, Matthies the Fortunate, who lived on the isle of Föhr, just off the coast of Denmark.[1]

From Sag Harbor, it's a brief ride to the coast and Peter Matthiessen's home in Sagaponack, a modest two-story wood structure tucked in the middle of about six acres of land that is bordered by trees and hedges and surrounded by potato fields. The driveway runs to what feels like the back of the house but is actually the main entrance, on whose brick porch sits a finback whale's gigantic skull, found by Matthiessen one day while walking on the ocean beach. Inside, the house has a worn, comfortable feeling, the wide pine floor of the living room strewn with rugs, an old oriental covering the coffee table-sofa area. Books are piled upon the gateleg table behind the sofa, apparently duty manuscripts waiting for comment or blurb, one a review copy of an African adventure. There are issues of the *New Yorker, Audubon*, and *Condé Nast Traveller*, at which Matthiessen's wife, Maria, works as an editor. The central fireplace is tiered brick, each level a resting place for curios from around the world, such as an African mask and tiny carved animals. Behind the fireplace is an open bar with plenty of bottles. The room has no television, but rather a stereo with turntable and compact disc player and some classical records and discs. The walls are grey-stained wood, giving the place a seaside, driftwood flavor. Matthiessen later told me he used old orange crates for the walls, one of which is covered with photographs of the Kurelu tribe of New Zealand. A sliding door leads to the U-shaped courtyard.

Matthiessen and his house seem one. He is wearing old jeans and a green sweater with at least three prominent holes. He is tall, wirily strong, and has the rugged, rumpled good looks of an adventurer, a real-life Indiana Jones. His age is easily belied by his athletic condition and calm energy. His gaze is direct and his attention full to each word of conversation, giving the impression of someone with great powers of concentration.

Matthiessen writes in a one-room workshop to the east of and behind the main house. This study is filled with mementos of his travels around the world—shells from the seven seas, arrows from Peru, feathers from Tanzania—as well as a computer, a printer, and books. The journeys are all there in miniature and emblem: the search for the great white shark that he recounted in *Blue Meridian*, the turtling adventure out of the Cayman Islands that inspired *Far Tortuga*, the Harvard-Peabody expedition to the outbacks of New Guinea that he told about in *Under the Mountain Wall*. To the west of the main house is an old barn, now converted into a zendo, where Matthiessen leads a Zen meditation group. The Matthiessen property lies only about a half mile from Sagaponack Beach, and on this wintry day the ocean frolicked and spumed as we walked its vacant sandy coast and talked over its periodic crescendo of surf.[2] After the visit, my trip south entailed no more ferry transport, but it did take me across the Verrazano Narrows Bridge, whose construction was begun in 1959, the very year a freighter with Matthiessen on board set off for South America through the neck of water the bridge would span. Out of the car window, the skyline of Manhattan, Matthiessen's birthplace, shone prominently in the pale light of dusk. Matthiessen's life, like that of his Manhattan-born, Long Island–residing predecessor, Walt Whitman, has been surrounded by water. There is the ancestral connection with the island of Föhr. And Matthiessen himself was taken to Fishers Island within a fortnight of his birth. Water also has carried him upon his many voyages, and the fantasy of island living has always haunted him. In fact, one of the two remaining nonfiction books Matthiessen wants to write is a series of island pieces called *The Search for an Island*, which will deal with the philosophical appeal of island living. "O madly the sea pushes upon the land," wrote Whitman, "With love, with love."

Peter Matthiessen was born on 22 May 1927, the second of three children, between older sister Mary Seymour and brother George Carey, to Erard A. Matthiessen and the former Elizabeth Carey. His father was a prominent architect in New York City and a trustee of the National Audubon Society. Matthiessen's lifelong interest in wildlife, which he shares with his brother, began in his Connecticut childhood with a snake collection. This accumulation grew progressively larger and more exotic until Mrs. Matthiessen discovered that the menagerie included seven copperheads and ordered that the collection be dispersed. Outdoor interests fostered by the boys' father included skiing, fishing, and hunting. Matthiessen fondly remembers the deep-sea fishing trips off Montauk Point with his father during the preadolescent years. Writing in *Men's Lives*, he says about Montauk, "I cannot see that high promontory of land with its historic lighthouse without a stirring of excitement and affection."[3] Matthiessen would dedicate his *Blue Meridian*, the account of a search for the great white shark, to his brother Carey, who pursued a career as a marine biologist.

The Matthiessens were well-off, maintaining a house overlooking the Hudson River, a summer house on Fishers Island, and a comfortable apartment at 1165 Fifth Avenue that faced Central Park, around the corner from St. Bernard's School. The latter address was also the home of George Plimpton, Matthiessen's classmate at St. Bernard's and later the editor of the *Paris Review*. It was a world of nannies and chauffeurs, an upbringing of privilege and taste, in which small boys were considered young gentlemen—although Peter and Carey got into trouble with such stunts as dropping water bombs on sidewalk targets from the living room windows. In a recent autobiographical essay, Matthiessen reminisces about the bittersweet experience of growing up in New York as a child of privilege, admitting to "a lot of rich-boy fun, brushing past the street poor with the cool callousness one must cultivate to avoid the discomforts of guilt, pity or distress."[4] Yet uneasiness with the life of unearned privilege grew quickly in the young Matthiessen, causing internal as well as family tension.

Though his family was Episcopalian, religion seems to have had little effect upon Matthiessen's early years, despite a lifelong fascination with cathedrals and church music. At the Hotchkiss School in rural Lakeville, Connecticut, he had some disciplinary problems, being headstrong and resistant to authority. Concerning this period, Matthiessen would later say, "My formative years left me unformed; despite kind parents, superior schooling, and all the orderly advantages, I remained disorderly." Notwithstanding the jumble, he was able to make a significant decision: "By the time I was sixteen, I had determined that I would write. Strange callow pieces with my byline were already appearing in the school publications. . . ."[5]

After prep school, with World War II nearing an end, Matthiessen, like his character Charlie Stark in *Raditzer*, enlisted in the navy (his father was a navy Lieutenant Commander, whose architectural and engineering skills were employed in the design of military weaponry). Peter was stationed at Pearl Harbor during 1945–46. He applied for sea duty, but was assigned instead to the base laundry. He wrote sports articles for the *Honolulu Advertiser*, managed the navy's Golden Gloves team, and rose to the rank of Ships Service Laundryman Third Class, before an altercation with the Shore Patrol caused him to be broken back to Seaman First Class. While in the navy, Matthiessen had one of the most memorable and seminal moments of his life. He recounts it as part of his spiritual evolution in *The Snow Leopard*: "One night in 1945, on a Navy vessel in Pacific storm, my relief on bow watch, seasick, failed to appear, and I was alone for eight hours in a maelstrom of wind and water, noise and iron; again and again, waves crashed across the deck, until water, air, and iron became one. Overwhelmed, exhausted, all thought and emotion beaten out of me, I lost my sense of self, the heartbeat I heard was the heart of the world, I breathed with the mighty risings and declines of the earth, and this evanescence seemed less frightening than exalting."[6] In a sense, all of his later voyages, both physical and spiritual, can be seen as Matthiessen's desire to recapture this sense of oneness with the universe, experienced significantly on the high seas.

Matthiessen returned from navy service in the autumn of 1946 too late to enroll in college. As a result of his being "considered an undesirable at home," he moved in with his mother's Aunt Bess in her New York apartment and attended night lectures at the New School for Social Research ("NY," 70). It was not a happy time. As Matthiessen recalls, "That fall and winter, my formerly uproarious and heedless nature turned dark and moody. Brooding, lonely, aching with romantic longings for unfettered 'real life,' I had developed a small drinking problem. . ." Fortunately, a kindly and forceful elevator man buttonholed him as he was taking a bag of booze up to the apartment and delivered a harangue that shook Matthiessen out of what he now calls his "disgusting self-indulgent melancholia" ("NY," 70).

The Hotchkiss School had been founded to prepare young men for Yale, and Matthiessen, after his navy stint and his brief period of lostness in New York, helped fulfill the founder's intention when he entered the university where his father had gone before him. While at Yale, Matthiessen deepened his commitment to writing, becoming an English major and a columnist for the *Yale Daily News*, to which he contributed hunting and fishing articles. He also took courses in zoology and ornithology, grounding his interest in nature with knowledge of its laws. Taking his junior year abroad, Matthiessen attended a branch of the New School for Social Research at the Sorbonne in Paris, where he met Patsy Southgate, a Smith junior also abroad for the year, who would later become his wife. Matthiessen's writing career was set in motion when a story he had written in a creative writing class—recommended to the *Atlantic Monthly* by John Farrar of Farrar, Straus—was accepted and won the *Atlantic* Prize for 1951. Following graduation, Matthiessen was hired at Yale as an instructor of creative writing, during which time he married Patsy Southgate, the daughter of a State Department diplomat.

It wasn't quite Scott and Zelda, but life did have a glow. Patsy Southgate was striking, in the description of a contemporary, "a small, lovely, vivacious blonde with pale blue eyes and a marvelous figure, and all the boys of twenty-six were in love with her."[7] Matthiessen's *Atlantic Monthly* success was doubled by the magazine's acceptance of another story, "The Fifth Day," which would appear in September 1951. Like other young American writers, he decided to return to Paris to live and write, distancing the influences of home and family and pursuing the undeniable attractions of the artist's life abroad. So in 1951 Patsy and Peter, for $21 a month, took a simple but airy apartment on the Rue Perceval, a small back street near the railroad tracks in Montparnasse.

In Paris he began to meet other Americans with literary ambitions. One such was Harold Humes, who had recently been expelled from MIT for sneaking a girl into a dorm and who was now hustling chess in the cafés where he and Matthiessen met. Another was William Styron, who called on Matthiessen and became a frequent guest at his "modest but lovely apartment."[8] The arrival in Paris of what Irwin Shaw (then in his late thirties and at the height of his literary fame) called "the tall young men" had begun. Matthiessen quickly became a central figure in the group that included his old St. Bernard's classmate George Plimpton, Styron, James Baldwin, Humes, Ben Bradlee, and Terry Southern; Matthiessen's apartment with its high ceilings and terrace and sunlight was where everyone would convene at 5 p.m. to drink and converse. By six, as Gay Talese recounts, the room would be floating in Dutch gin and absinthe (Talese, 106).

Humes, by all accounts, was the most inventive and unpredictable of the lot, and it was he and Matthiessen who hatched the idea of the *Paris Review*. The concept was honed in later discussions with George Plimpton, Thomas Guinzburg, William Pene du Bois, John Train, and Styron in the cafés of Paris. The name came from Matthiessen, who had invited Plimpton to Paris from Cambridge, England, to be editor-in-chief. Matthiessen was the first fiction editor of the magazine, which, amazingly in the mercurial world of small magazines, survives to this day. Both his and Plimpton's names still appear at the top of the masthead, although Matthiessen is no longer active in the editorial work.

Unquestionably, there was a great deal of hubris in these tall young pretenders to the roles of arbiters and transmitters of literary taste, especially since Styron was the only published novelist among them, and he had published only one novel. Fresh from the triumph of *Lie Down in Darkness* (1951) when he arrived on Matthiessen's Parisian doorstep in the spring of 1952, Styron was disconcerted that the younger writer "did not display the deference I thought fitting to the situation" (Styron, 249). Nevertheless, Matthiessen had published two short stories, and, in 1952, a third story was accepted, this one by *Botteghe Oscure*. This magazine was then, according to Janet Flanner (Genet), "the leading European literary review and probably the only important one in four languages—Italian, French, English, and American—addressed to the literati of Rome, Paris, London, and New York."[9]

The *Paris Review* itself appeared in 1953 with a manifesto by Styron, who proclaimed that it "would strive to give predominant space to the fiction and poetry of both established and new writers, rather than to people who use words like *Zeitgeist*."[10] The intent was clearly to reverse the predominance of criticism over original writing that the *Review* staff perceived in other literary magazines. More important, however, than the content of Styron's piece was its tone. He had at first written it as a preface, but finally he put it in the form of a letter to the editor, apparently a bit disconcerted by the number of editorial changes wrought upon his original version. So, in the new form, while he was still speaking for the editorial staff—as Advisory Editor explaining the rationale of the new venture—Styron's tone was personal, relaxed, and unpretentious. The editors seemed to be saying: send us good fiction and good poetry, and don't stand on ceremony or lean on jargon—directions that have guided the periodical's policy over the course of its long and healthy life.

The *Paris Review* was not the only Matthiessen offspring of 1953. In March, his son Luke was born in Paris. The following summer, the family of three shared a house with the Styrons at Ravello on the Amalfi Drive, where the couples "played tennis and interminable word games, talked for long hours about writers and writing, and swam in the then pellucid and unpolluted Mediterranean" (Styron, 250). In August 1953, with the *Paris Review* founded, a novel written, and another plotted, Matthiessen sailed home to America with his wife and infant son on the *Andrea Doria*. They settled in East Hampton, Long Island, where he became a commercial fisherman to support his writing.

The move back to the states, after a period of literary incubation abroad, was a common one for the 1950s expatriates, as it had been for the writers of the 1920s. Paris in the mid-fifties was hardly hospitable toward its American guests. While some would stay on in permanent exile, most "would go back to New York," as Malcolm Cowley noted about the 1920s generation, "then settle in a Connecticut farmhouse with their books, a portable typewriter and the best intentions."[11] Indeed, Styron would go back to a Connecticut farmhouse, and Matthiessen would go to Long Island because he was, in his own words, "unsuited to urban work and . . . sought a leaner way of life outdoors" (*ML*, 56). Fishing provided that. Matthiessen was able to structure a life that suited his physical needs yet still left time for his writing. He could fish (scalloping, clamming, haul seining) in spring and fall, run a charter boat during the summer, and write when the weather was bad and during the winter. The balance was ideal. In a 1986 interview, Matthiessen called this "the happiest time of my life—not in terms of writing, necessarily, but the life really suited me to a T."[12]

In 1954, Matthiessen's daughter Sara Carey was born, and his first book, *Race Rock*, was published to generally positive reviews. The following year, his second novel, *Partisans*, was received respectfully but less favorably, and neither book made money. So, Matthiessen began to think of other alternatives. One senses that he never intended the commercial fishing to go on indefinitely; and, in any case, the seasoned fishermen themselves were having a hard time making ends meet. His marriage became strained—he felt he had settled down and planted roots too early. In August 1956, when he was invited to join a shorthanded haul-seining crew, he declined: "I shook my head; my days as a commercial fisherman were over. My marriage had disintegrated, my old fishing partners were scattering, and my friend Jackson [Pollock], driving drunk, had destroyed himself and a young woman passenger when he lost control on the Springs-Fireplace Road" (*ML*, 150). Matthiessen admits that he had lost "all heart" for charter fishing, so he sold his boat and "a beautiful piece of woods" in Amagansett where he had planned to build a house.

Although his divorce was not formalized until 1958, by the end of 1956 Matthiessen was off on his own, beginning the explorations of wild places that have become his hallmark. He says, "I was single again, and for the next five years did the world wandering that I should have gotten out of my system before marrying people and having children" (*World Authors*, 957). The first of these journeys was within his native country. He packed his green Ford convertible with books on wildlife, a shotgun, and a sleeping bag, and drove off to visit every wildlife refuge in the United States. The project, like so many in Matthiessen's life, has an immensity of proportions about it. At twenty-six, he founded a literary magazine; at twenty-nine, he crisscrossed the country to write a history of wildlife in America. The two acts respond to the opposite poles of his personality, the civilized/ intellectual and the wild/physical, just as these polarities are motifs in his early novels. It is the same duality that was generated by the fishing-writing balance of his previous years on Long Island. And it is the same duality that is mirrored in the Matthiessen ancestry, with its direct line to the legendary 17th-century whaling captain Matthies the Fortunate (who took an astonishing 373 whales in his lifetime), and with literary forebears such as the 19th-century novelist Charlotte Matthiessen (author of *Rungoldt*) and 20th-century critic F. O. Matthiessen, a first cousin of Peter's father.

The books he took west were a practical necessity, for the only formal training Matthiessen had to fall back on was his few college courses in the sciences. In a *Publishers Weekly* interview, he admitted, "I'm not really trained in any of the disciplines; I'm what the 19th century would call a generalist—I have a lot of slack information, and for my work it's been extremely helpful" (Smith, 241). Also extremely helpful, and something that cannot be taught or learned, are his Thoreau-like powers of observation, for he relies heavily in his nonfiction on first-hand experience. He trusts his own eyes and ears, but he nevertheless submits his observations to the scrutiny of more scientifically trained acquaintances, as is obvious from the number of acknowledgments in the front of all his nonfiction books.

Wildlife in America was published in 1959 after three years of travel, research, and writing. During this period, Matthiessen managed to support his family with income from book advances, magazine pieces, and editing. He kept his hand in fiction, and three of his stories appeared in magazines. He also began his relationship with the *New Yorker* and its editor, William Shawn, a relationship that would prove most influential on the course of his career. His first *New Yorker* article was a report on the Parisian trial of Yvonne Chevallier for the murder of her husband in 1951, which had been researched by Ben Bradlee when they were in Paris. While abroad they had shown the piece to Irwin Shaw, long a *New Yorker* contributor, who wrote a note of recommendation to be sent with the manuscript to Shawn; but when Bradlee and Matthiessen saw how tepid and patronizing the recommendation was, they decided it would hurt rather than help their chances of publication and didn't include it. As it turned out, the account was accepted on its own merit, though not without some controversy. An indication of the young Matthiessen's proprietary confidence in his own writing ability occurred when Matthiessen got wind through a *New Yorker* researcher that the magazine had recast the entire piece without his permission, putting it in chronological order with new connecting material. His immediate instructions to his agent, Bernice Baumgarten, were to withdraw the article and bomb the place. Meanwhile, a check for $1800 was making its way through the mail and into Matthiessen's hands, the largest payment he had received for anything yet written. Despite his agent's pleading, Matthiessen returned the check, advising Shawn that he'd accept payment only if his name was removed from the piece, suggesting they put the editor's name as author. Shawn asked the offended young writer to come see him about the matter. This was their first meeting.

Matthiessen recalls the legendary corner office "with the light from the window behind him [Shawn] shining through his ears, his little brown paper lunch bag on the desk. He was very kind and gracious, suggesting that the editor and I ought to be able to work this out together. I said that I doubted the editor would work with me after reading my letter. William Shawn replied, 'Mr. Matthiessen, I took the precaution of not showing your letter to that editor.'"[13] As it turned out, the editor had already gotten wind of the letter, and it proved to be a tense few days of work, but a compromise was reached and the piece appeared as "Annals of Crime" (1 Nov. 1958). Matthiessen's work was never again treated so cavalierly by the magazine. Subsequently, the *New Yorker* sponsored Matthiessen's 1959 trip to the wilderness areas of South America, a trip that took him up, down, and across the continent and resulted in a series of three pieces, combined into *The Cloud Forest* (1961).

Observing this time in Matthiessen's life, one sees the pattern of his days fishing and writing at East Hampton magnified into greater stretches of activity and writing. The year 1959 was largely consumed by his South American trip, and in 1960 he bought very inexpensively what has become his permanent home on six acres of land in Sagaponack, Long Island, an old farming community that later would attract many other writers and artists. The following year saw him off on the Harvard-Peabody expedition to New Guinea, with visits en route to the Sudan, East Africa, Nepal, and Southeast Asia. In 1962, he wrote and published *Under the Mountain Wall*, based on the New Guinea contact with the Kurelu, a tribe previously untouched by Western civilization.

No man travels to so many parts of the world without seeking something, and Matthiessen had embarked on an inner as well as an outer journey. While in South America, he experimented with a jungle hallucinogen, *yage* or *ayahuasca*, which convinced him that such drugs might lead to a different and enlightened way of perceiving reality. For the next ten years, he used them regularly, mostly LSD but also mescaline and psilocybin. When I asked him if any of his books were written under the influence of drugs, his reply was that only the drug/dream sequence in *At Play in the Fields of the Lord* was directly influenced by drugs. After one terrifying trip on a peasant form of heroin in Cambodia, Matthiessen says he "treated drugs with more respect, working seriously with a renegade psychiatrist who was making bold, early experiments in the use of hallucinogens in therapy. My companion was a girl named Deborah Love, who was adrift on the same instinctive search" (*SL*, 44).

Matthiessen had first met Love when he was living in Paris, but their second meeting was coincidental, almost ten years later on Sagaponack Beach. Matthiessen had been hand seining in shallow water when an attractive woman came over with her little girl to see what he was doing. Before long, he and the mother were talking, and he asked her out. Not until later did Love remind him of their earlier meeting in Paris. Deborah Love became Matthiessen's second wife in 1963. He adopted her daughter, Rue, and fathered her son, Alexander, in 1964.

Matthiessen continued his travels to various parts of the world in spite of the tensions in his marriage that his long absences caused. In 1964, he joined an expedition to Nunivak Island in the Bering Sea to bring some specimens of the near-extinct musk ox to Alaska for breeding. The experience was reported in the *New Yorker* (6 Feb. 1966) and expanded into *Oomingmak* (1967). In 1967, again sponsored by the magazine, he was off in search of the green turtle on an old converted schooner out of Grand

Cayman Island, resulting in another *New Yorker* piece (28 Oct. 1967) and ultimately in his great novel, *Far Tortuga* (1975). In late 1968, Matthiessen visited Cesar Chavez in California and wrote about him and his work in a *New Yorker* profile (21, 28 June 1969) as well as in a book, *Sal Si Puedes* (1969).

Returning home from a seven-month stay in Africa in August 1968, Matthiessen was surprised to find in his Sagaponack driveway "three inscrutable small men" who turned out to be Japanese Zen masters. They had been invited by Matthiessen's wife, who had turned away from drugs and towards this form of enlightenment. This was Matthiessen's first contact with Zen, and the seed would grow. By this time, Matthiessen himself had also abandoned his psychedelic experimentation. As he explains it, "the magic show grows boring" (*SL*, 47). One December weekend in 1969, he accompanied his wife on a *sesshin*, a silent retreat. Although Matthiessen found the *sesshin* painful, masochistic, even boring, he carried away something with him on his next trip. This undersea search for the great white shark, with world famous diver Peter Gimbel, resulted in Gimbel's film "Blue Water, White Death" and Matthiessen's book *Blue Meridian* (1971). While on the expedition, Matthiessen found himself doing Zen meditation daily.

When he next returned home, a reconciliation took place ("my wife and I at last embraced each other's failings"[14]) and Deborah invited him to join her on a visit to the tract of land that would become the site of the first Zen monastery built in America. There Matthiessen met the Zen monk who would become his teacher, Soen Nakagawa-roshi. During his early apprenticeship of 1970–72, despite the earlier reconciliation, Matthiessen and his wife continued to have their ups and downs and reached a mutual decision to divorce in the summer of 1971. Then strangely and mysteriously, as Matthiessen tells it, "The very next day, acting on an imperious command, I made a commitment to D, this time for good. She understood; sipping coffee in the sun, she merely nodded" (*SL*, 77). Just a few months later, Deborah felt the first symptoms of the cancer that would end her life in January 1972. The couple's final reconciliation and resurgence of love coincided with their Zen devotion in a swirl of emotional intensity that climaxed in Deborah's emergence in a state of grace from what was thought to be a terminal coma. Her last word was "Peter."

In November 1973, Matthiessen embarked on a 250-mile trek across the high passes of the Himalayas in pilgrimage to the Crystal Monastery, an ancient Buddhist shrine, with biologist George Schaller. The trip was many things to Matthiessen: a spiritual journey, a grief observed, an exploration of the rarest parts of nature. Schaller was interested in studying the peculiar blue sheep of Nepal, and both men hoped to see the elusive and mysterious snow leopard. In a real sense, the experience was Matthiessen's farewell to his late wife and a working through of his own lingering sadness. About this aspect, he would write in his journal of the trip: "In the autumnal melancholy I remember France, in the years that I lived there, still in love with my first wife. One day in Paris, I met Deborah Love, whom I was to marry ten years later. And now, in different ways, those life-filled creatures are both gone. I hurry with the river" (*SL*, 291–92).

In 1974, Matthiessen was elected to the National Institute of Arts and Letters, and that year he also set about finishing a novel he had been working on for almost a decade. *Far Tortuga* was published to considerable acclaim in 1975, many reviewers singling it out as his most daring achievement as a writer. Matthiessen has always been enormously productive during periods of time packed with activity, travel, and upheaval. Besides his books and *New Yorker* pieces, he has continued over the years to write articles for magazines like *Audubon*, *Geo*, and the *New York Times Magazine*. Matthiessen himself says he has never experienced what most writers know as writer's block. And William Styron has called him "one of the most industrious writers alive" (Styron, 250). When I asked Matthiessen how he was able to write so prolifically, his response was: "I don't know about prolific. I work pretty hard. Always have. It's normal for me to put in about fifty hours a week." Generally he writes from 8:30 to 12:30 in the morning, is back at his desk with a cup of coffee from about 1:00 to 3:00 in the afternoon, and usually works in the evening as well. Writing is a six-days-a-week activity, sometimes seven if he decides to do a little on Sunday.

The years between 1972 and 1976 were a time of intense Zen practice for Matthiessen. He frequently attended eight-day retreats including *zazen*, or the practice of sitting meditation that seeks to eliminate the separation between self and object. His daily schedule also included time for such meditation. In fact, the rigors of this long cross-legged sitting in the lotus position caused such soreness in his right knee that it occasionally required aspirin, heat pads, and liniment. Matthiessen writes that after four years of such fervor, "the early, infatuated days of my Zen practice had come to an end, the flowers were just flowers once again" (*NHDR*, 64). For more than two years after the 4 July 1976 inaugural *sesshin* at the Dai Bosatsu Zendo in the Catskills, he stayed away, polishing his Himalayan journals in *The Snow Leopard* (1978), which took the place of "the intense sesshin attendance of the past four years" (*NHDR*, 67).

Part of Matthiessen's inner journey during this period involved a shifting from the Rinzai to the Soto sect of Zen. Soto Zen traditionally emphasizes "just sitting" (*shikan-taza*) over the use of gnomic riddles and anecdotes (koan study) as a way of enlightenment. It also differs from the more Spartan Rinzai tradition in that it lacks the latter's rigor, precision, and the physical discipline of the "warning stick" (*keisaku*). When a Soto teacher, the Brooklyn-born Tetsugen-sensei, led a *sesshin* in June 1979, in the New York area, Matthiessen assisted. The following year Tetsugen founded the Zen Community of New York and became Matthiessen's new formal teacher. It was he who officiated at Matthiessen's wedding, in 1980, to Maria Eckhart, a beautiful woman, born in Tanzania, whom Matthiessen had met in New York City in 1968. A year after his marriage, Matthiessen was ordained as a Zen monk by a Soto Master he had studied under in Los Angeles, Taizan Maezumi-roshi, who shaved Matthiessen's head and spoke of this commitment as even more important than marriage, which greatly displeased Matthiessen's wife.

After his ordination, Matthiessen became Tetsugen-sensei's first head monk, assisting with the New York Zen Community. In this role, he would travel with his master in 1982 to visit the ancient Soto Zen shrines of Japan, paying homage to the great teachers in this spiritual tradition, particularly the 13th-century master, Eihei Dogen. The account of this pilgrimage, as well as a history of Zen in America and a personal record of his spiritual commitment, is Matthiessen's *Nine-Headed Dragon River* (1985).

Predictably, Matthiessen's writing output in the 1980s has not faltered. *Sand Rivers*, an account of his trip to Tanzania's Selous Game Preserve and the East African plains, was published in 1981. And, as a result of his continuous research and travel among the American Indians since 1975, Matthiessen brought out two books, *In the Spirit of Crazy Horse* (1983) and *Indian Country* (1984). The former, a controversial defense of the young Ojibwa-Sioux Leonard Peltier, questionably convicted for killing two FBI agents, was enjoined from distribution until the resolution of a $24 million lawsuit filed by former Governor William Janklow of South Dakota and a $25 million lawsuit filed by FBI agent David Price. Both cases were resolved in Matthiessen and Viking's favor in 1990, when the U. S. Supreme Court declined to review Price's appeal and when the South Dakota Supreme Court upheld a lower court's dismissal of Janklow's suit. In 1986, another book of advocacy for threatened ways of life, *Men's Lives*, was published. In it Matthiessen recounts the ways of the commercial fishermen of the South Fork of Long Island, whose livelihood is more threatened by misguided legislation than by changing ecology. Matthiessen agrees with Albert Camus that it is part of the writer's responsibility to speak for those who cannot speak for themselves; it is in that spirit that he has championed the causes of Cesar Chavez, Leonard Peltier, the American Indian, and the baymen of the South Fork.

While Matthiessen is perhaps more visible as a nature and travel writer than as a novelist, reporting on the wild to the civilized, he has returned in recent years to fiction, which he considers his most important work and on which he intends to focus most of his energy from now on. *On the River Styx and Other Stories* is a collection of his short fiction from his first *Atlantic* story to his 1989 work. His sixth novel, *Killing Mister Watson*, is set in remote southwestern Florida and is based upon a true incident in 1910 involving the execution of an admired but feared citizen by his neighbors. Matthiessen also returned briefly to teaching, offering a creative-writing course for advanced students at Yale in the spring of 1989.

Matthiessen still lives on the same property he bought in 1960 in Sagaponack. Because of the area's intense development in recent years, he worries about the disappearance of the open fields through which we walked that cold January day of my visit in 1989. He pointed to the new construction along nearby Sagaponack Pond and cited the increasing financial pressure on the potato farmers and others to cash in on the spiraling prices. One senses that he himself will never sell, for the place suits Matthiessen, with its wild sea-spumed shore, its bird-rich marshes, and its stark, austere winter beauty.

Matthiessen's property is surrounded by a large privet hedge. Off to the side of the house is his office, a former children's playhouse. On the other side of the main house, with its large comfortable living room and bright roomy kitchen, sits the zendo, a place of meditation that allows Matthiessen to serve the Zen Community of New York as its priest/teacher. It seemed symbolic, the winter day I visited, that the zendo was occupied by only one creature, a small saw-whet owl that the Matthiessens were hoping would recuperate after flying into their car window. While I was there, Maria's call to the local vet was returned with advice about its care. Matthiessen's Zen embraces all creatures, and his life in Sagaponack has a harmony of the natural and the spiritual about it. He still travels, but less so. And, at least for now, his mind is more involved with flights of the imagination than with treks afoot or journeys by sea.

Chapter Two
Paris and the Writer's Life
Race Rock, Partisans, Raditzer

The 1950s and the Second Line of American Expatriates

Although Peter Matthiessen had moved back to America by the time his first book, *Race Rock*, appeared in 1954, he had written it in Paris, and his two years living there between 1951 and 1953 indelibly influenced his vision of the writer's role. "To be young and in Paris is often a heady experience," remarked William Styron, who met Matthiessen there in 1951 when he was twenty-seven and Matthiessen was twenty-five years old (Styron, 297). These two men, along with a number of expatriates such as James Baldwin, Richard Wright, Irwin Shaw, George Plimpton, and others, constituted a second generation of American writers who called France their home—at least for a while—during the 1950s. Gay Talese, who wrote about this continental scene, says that Matthiessen's apartment was "as much a meeting place for the young American literati as was Gertrude Stein's apartment in the Twenties" (Talese, 106). Like Hemingway, Fitzgerald, Cummings, and Dos Passos, who came to live in Europe after World War I, the second line of American expatriates arrived in Paris after World War II, drawn by the magnetism of the city's literary associations, its beauty, its centrality, and its air of liberation. It was also a cheap place to live for a young writer who was not ready to settle down and get a "real job" back in middle America. Ironically, Malcolm Cowley, who published his chronicle of the 1920s, *Exile's Return*, in the very year that Matthiessen settled in Paris, claims in his prologue that "the young writers of the present age aren't young or foolish enough [to live the bohemian life abroad] and, once out of college and the army, settle down too safely to earning a sensible living" (Cowley, 12). Cowley could not have known about Matthiessen, Styron, and most of the others because they were just setting out on their literary and geographic journeys.

Paris was everything that Matthiessen needed to launch his career as a writer. Paris was art. Paris was literature. Styron relates the story of a French landlady who, spying the translation by her young boarder of a French poem in a literary magazine, offered him a 2-percent decrease in his rent as a gesture of appreciation (Styron, 297). *Belles Lettres* was revered in Paris, and in this kind of atmosphere literary ambition was natural. The young Americans read voraciously and talked about books and writing over bread and cheese in the morning, during picnic lunches along the Seine, over drinks in the cafés and bars of Montparnasse, and over more drinks in Matthiessen's third-floor flat, which quickly became the gathering spot of the young expatriate crowd. "It was an extremely bohemian apartment," recalls Matthiessen's then wife, Patsy Southgate. "It was an artist's studio, a great big atelier with vines growing over the windows, and a coal stove, and it was freezing cold—just what you wanted if you were twenty-three years old and living in Paris."[1]

Out of such discussions at Peter's flat and at one particularly smoky bar, Le Chaplain (whose Algerian owner liked the Americans and their literary talk), evolved the *Paris Review.* By all accounts the inspiration for the review was Matthiessen's, although he and Harold Humes were cofounders. Doc Humes, as everyone knew him, had bought out a magazine devoted to covering restaurants and Paris nightlife, called *Kiosk,* renamed it *Paris News Post,* and decided to run a short story in each issue, enlisting Matthiessen as fiction editor. As Matthiessen remembers:

The first story I got for him was Terry Southern's first story, "The Sun and the Still-Born Stars,". . . a very good story, one of the best Terry ever wrote. And when I saw that story in this flimsy magazine, I thought, If we're going to do good stories, let's start a real magazine, with fiction by young writers, and interviews with famous writers to carry the fiction. Doc wanted to be the head of it, and I didn't, I just wanted to take care of the fiction and work on my first novel, but it didn't take long to realize that the magazine just wasn't going to work with Doc in charge. Lovable and intelligent though he was, he couldn't work with people. So I got in touch with [George] Plimpton, who was at Cambridge in England. I knew he had run the Harvard [literary] magazine and I asked him to come over to Paris and run this one. He said sure—can't imagine why—and it ruined his whole life. (Quoted in Shnayerson, 210–11)

According to Styron, Plimpton, with two green bottles of absinthe under his arms, burst into "a glum gathering desultorily testing names" for the new magazine at the Matthiessen apartment (Styron, 297). The other founders of the magazine were Thomas Guinzburg, William Pene du Bois, and John Train, but it was Matthiessen who came up with the name that would stick. Writing was important, and the name chosen for the journal indicates the significance of the city itself to their literary endeavor. Even when most of the founders had moved back to America, the review's name and an editorial office in Paris would remain.

Paris was new magazines, and Paris was a tradition of literary experimentalism, directly inherited from the American exiles of the 1920s. Styron admits that while these members of the lost generation did not have "exclusive hold on our attention . . . it has to be conceded that rarely has such a group of literary figures had the impact that these writers have had on their immediate descendents and successors" (Styron, 90). And the principal effect of this impact on a writer such as Matthiessen at the start of his writing career was in the area of language. In fact, all of the American writers starting their careers in Europe in the 1950s became acutely conscious of style, a direct inheritance from Hemingway, Fitzgerald, Faulkner, and Wolfe, who as a group had distinguished themselves by "an original way of combining words (a style, a 'voice') and utter commitment to a dream . . . of being the lords of language."[2] This commitment to language was bolstered by the moral fervor with which style has always been approached in Paris, where *le mot juste* has an air not only of righteousness, but of justification as well.

Paris was also freedom, both from the pressures of achieving instant popular success and from the constraints of American domesticity. More significantly, it was freedom from the immediacy of one's early surroundings, allowing a writer the requisite distance to put the experiences of one's youth in perspective. It is no wonder that in his first novel, Matthiessen wrote about the wild shore off New England's coast, a shore with which he was distinctly familiar from his fifteen youthful summers spent on Fishers Island. In Paris three decades earlier, Hemingway had written about a remote stream in northern Michigan where he had fished as a boy. As Cowley notes about the 1920s writers, "It was not by accident that their early books were almost all nostalgic, full of the wish to recapture some remembered thing" (Cowley, 9).

Paris was also the larger world, *the* cosmopolitan city, and as such, an initiation into the foreign. Matthiessen had, of course, been to Paris as a student and had been stationed at Pearl Harbor at the end of World War II. In fact, most of the second line of American writers abroad had their first introduction to the larger world through military service in the war, just as the 1920s generation had had theirs on the battlefields and in the ambulances of World War I. To visit, however, is not to live. Settling in Europe allowed the writers the expanse of imagination provided by living in a foreign culture. That Paris was the quintessentially foreign city provided the writers with an enlarged vision of the world. Even after they returned to the States and settled in New York or Connecticut, like the writers before them in the 1920s, the second line would carry with them a vision made more global by the years abroad. Matthiessen, in particular, would travel to many parts of the world, and his imagination was poised thereafter to sympathize with the alien and the remote.

The economy, style, and experimentalism of Matthiessen's first three novels, then, were fostered by his residence in Paris during the incubation of his literary career. Paris liberated him, as it had other American writers, from the early and damning constraints of achieving immediate commercial success and conforming to existing literary categories. Paris allowed him to breathe the pure air of art, which resulted in finely crafted novels, whose language reviewers praised more consistently than any other quality. Paris gave Matthiessen the necessary distance from his past to write serious novels, resolving issues in his own life and introducing lifelong themes of his work to come.

The Novels

The three early novels are truncated bildungsromans, each with a young man who is wellborn and educated as its central character. Instead of the labored narrative of personal development, however, Matthiessen's books concentrate on a particular situation in the character's young manhood, reaching into his past background only for incidents that bear on the terms of the present. In each case, the young man must choose between competing allegiances: the life of privilege in which he has been raised, or the life of struggle that he comes to know. He must either accept what is given or strive for what is unknown. The individual novels deal with various facets of this predicament: *Race Rock* focuses on the question of inheritance (How does one deal with what has been provided by parents and circumstances?), *Partisans* on the question of ideals (What should one do in the world?), and *Raditzer* on the question of outsiders (How does one deal with those who are utterly different?). The books sequentially address the concerns of a typically privileged young man who is both sensitive and honest. He first asks, "What indeed have I been given?" Then, "What shall I do with it?" And finally, "What about those less privileged?" Like the rich young man in the gospel story who approaches Jesus about the requirements of his salvation, he idealistically questions, "What more must I do?" Within this larger search for bearings, the young man must respond to rival calls on his way of living: primitivism vs. civilization, marriage vs. freedom, parental ideals vs. one's own, and peer opinion vs. private vision.

Race Rock   In *Race Rock* (1954) the young man is George McConville, scion of Cyrus McConville and his considerable fortune. This includes a Wall Street investment firm and a summer estate on the New England coast at Shipman's Point, where George and his childhood friends Sam Rubicam, Eve Murphy, and Cady Shipman used to play together. It is 1952, and George is confronted by Eve with the news that she is pregnant by him, triggering what became labeled a crisis of identity in the 1960s, but in 1952 was simply thought of as a blue funk. When Sam, who had been briefly married to Eve, shows up, he and George get drunk and decide to go back to the days of youth by visiting the Point for a little weekend duck hunting. It is this weekend that focuses the immediate crisis, and it is made more climactic by the presence of two disturbing figures from George's boyhood, Daniel Barleyfield, a half-breed Indian, and Cady Shipman. Cady was always poorer than Sam and George, although he has reason to believe he should have been heir to the original Shipman land that was bought cheaply by Cyrus McConville. George, the child of plenty and the natural center of the group because he shares qualities with both Sam and Cady (who are antithetical and outrightly hostile to one another) frames the concerns of the novel by the choices he must make. He must resolve his allegiances to the two men, his doubt about making a commitment to Eve, and his discomfort with the implications of being a McConville.

Sam and Cady represent the contrary tugs of civilization and primitivism. They are opposites: the former intellectual, sophisticated, and cultured; the latter physical, shrewd, and brutal. From a Jungian point of view, Sam is George's persona, the stance he adopts in his normal accommodations with the world; Cady is George's shadow, his darker side that is socially unacceptable because of its raw and uncivilized passions. As we would expect, George is closer to Sam in all the noticeable ways: they are the best of friends, reading the same books, telling the same jokes, even sharing the same woman's love. George, however, is fascinated by Cady, who is from the other side of the tracks; he envies Cady's sense of self and his capability for action. Eve recognizes George's secret desire to be like Cady and confronts him with his own envy: "Isn't he the other person you wish you were, the craggy, outdoor type, the breath of the woods, the hard-bitten, laconic sage of the swampland, that you wish. . . " Before she can finish, George interrupts with, "I have never seen you so bitchy."[3] Later Sam also remarks to George on Cady's hold on him: "Everything you tell me about Cady is so macabre, it's as if you liked him for the very things that I detest in him. You're *proud* of his cruelty, in a way." And George lets down his denial long enough to admit that Cady "has a certain force I wouldn't mind having, do you know what I mean? He doesn't compromise every two seconds like the rest of us, he does what he pleases." "So do animals," retorts Sam (*RR*, 90–91).

In order to focus George's difficulty in integrating his animal-like side into his life, Matthiessen presents a flashback of the important boyhood incident of Percy Shipman's cat and its aftermath. Cady killed the tomcat and, when Sam scuffled with him over his cruelty, Cady took out his anger on Sam. George guiltily did not stand up to Cady and stop him from beating Sam and forcing Sam to lick his boots. After the beating, George stood over Sam glowering his scorn at Sam's weakness and disclaiming any responsibility. " 'Don't tell *me*. . . . Tell him'. . . . rebuking Sam for a cowardice shared between them, as if he were saying, if you want to hang around with Cady and me, Sam, you have to take care of yourself, because we're a pretty tough pair, Cady and me, we don't fool around with sissies" (*RR*, 91). George affects the tough-guy stance with Sam because he wants to avoid facing his own cowardice. In other words, he has aped Cady's manner, speaking "in a local accent like Cady's, standing over him [Sam] the way Cady had stood over him, as if by identifying himself with the voice and posture of the caretaker's son he might escape the lostness which the incident had brought to Sam" (*RR*, 91). But his imitation has no substance. Instead of acting out of his powerful, Cady-like shadow, George has followed an intellectualization of Cady's behavior. He is a sissy pretending he is a bully. His performance stems not from his shadow, but from his persona telling him how his shadow might act.

Matthiessen resolves George's important dilemma during the course of the three men's reunion weekend at the Point as adults in the autumn of 1952. The scene parallels the boyhood incident with the cat, exemplifying the novel's careful architectural scaffolding. As previously, Cady acts cruelly and sadistically. Instead of tormenting an animal, however, he turns to bigger game, instigating a round of Russian roulette, first pulling the trigger himself, then cajoling George and Sam into participating. After George, giving in to the pressure of both men, complies, Sam follows suit and crumbles in a heap of tears as he imagines himself shot. When both Sam and George realize that all the chambers were empty and that Cady had merely been playing with them, Sam charges and Cady responds by pummeling him. It is here that George reverses his childhood behavior and comes decisively to Sam's rescue, hitting Cady on the back of the head with the revolver's butt. In acting thus, George exorcises the demons of his duality, for he responds to the situation out of his shadow side, exerting a brutal and savage force from instinct, not from planning. Instead of pretending to be like Cady, as he had in his youth, for a brief moment he is Cady. Ironically, George gets in touch with his shadow by boldly attacking his shadow figure, Cady, thus dispelling his self-dissatisfaction. Afterward, George thinks, "now I am all alone, but at least I am no longer afraid" (*RR*, 253).

The larger resolution of the issue of civilization vs. primitivism is a synthetic one. George has not rejected his education or his friendship with Sam. In fact, he has protected Sam from the fists of Cady. On the other hand, he has done this only by violence, by catching hold of his primitive self and becoming, temporarily at least, one with it. In Jungian psychology, it is important that the shadow be recognized; otherwise, its force cannot be tapped and the individual will squander energy in the effort at denial. Matthiessen mirrors this Jungian synthesis, having his protagonist embrace his primitive side within the context of an altruistic, and therefore basically civilized, act.

George's dilemma about Eve and her pregnancy has more structural than thematic bearing on the story. It is the instigating crisis in George's life, forcing him into a weekend of soul-searching and confrontation with his duality about the Sam/Cady sides of himself and about his patrimonial inheritance. These are the deeper issues George must resolve, and once he does that, he is able to make a commitment to Eve. Eve, meanwhile, has aborted her pregnancy, and, after some soul-searching of her own, realizes she no longer loves George. When she and George face their new feelings at the end, it is with understanding. Still angry with him for his indecision, Eve nevertheless recognizes George's growth and respects him for it. The novel ends with the two forgivingly and comfortingly in each other's arms, albeit unromantically so.

More significant than the issue of commitment in marriage is that of inheritance. George's ambivalence about the privileges of his birthright surfaces frequently. He had been thinking of quitting McConville, Incorporated, before the immediate events of the weekend, feeling "the senselessness of his life, its lack of direction" (*RR*, 210) and complaining to Eve about "this sanctuary we lived in as children, and all the phony build-up to a life that doesn't exist, not any more, at least" (*RR*, 211). George ridicules his father as "the robber baron" and his mother as a cultural pretender "for the simple reason of her ancestry" (*RR*, 211), and he indicts his parents' generation for refusing to "recognize or understand the changes taking place in the world" (*RR*, 211).

Not until the climactic weekend, however, does George resolve his vague uneasiness by taking action. Both Cady and Daniel represent the dispossessed. Cady, as the bastard son of Barton Shipman, would have been the natural heir to what became the McConville estate. Instead, with none of the boyhood advantages of George or Sam, he became a caretaker like his legal father. Daniel, the grandson of an Indian chief, was found in the fields as a baby, adopted by Cyrus McConville, and given a place, a decidedly second-class indentured place, on the estate. In fact, when George returns for the duck hunting, he rebukes Daniel for calling him by his first name, suggesting that Daniel use "Mr. George." Only after Daniel's death, an indirect casualty of the Russian roulette foolishness, does George detach himself from his heritage, making a clean break with his privileged life. Seeing Daniel's body on the beach, he moans "with anger toward himself and toward what he represented of the world," his moan to be forever "a guardian angel against his past indifference." We are told that now George's "glass house had fallen" (RR, 281).

The theme of divestiture of the burdens of wealth is strengthened when George decides never to come back to the McConville estate. In fact, he resolves his lurking guilt toward Cady and his plight by offering him the house. On the symbolic level, George takes off all his clothes before rowing Daniel's skiff back to its mooring: "he drew off the gloved heavy garments one by one, until he was white and naked under the sun. His skin was alive with a clean glory he had not known since a child, a sense of beginnings, of infinite possibilities" (RR, 284).

In Race Rock Peter Matthiessen clearly was addressing issues in his own life through the story of George McConville. Matthiessen, unlike the other writers in Paris in the early 1950s, turned to a job involving hard physical work when he returned to the States, becoming a commercial fisherman and a charter boat captain. While he was doing this, however, he continued to write, synthesizing the Cady/Sam sides of his personality, a synthesis he would continue by writing about the many arduous and dangerous expeditions of his career. As for divestiture, Matthiessen's living abroad took on something of that nature, as did his not relying on family wealth. His account of his years fishing off the Long Island coast, Men's Lives, depicts somewhat close-to-the-bone financial circumstances. One cannot help but see George McConville's rowing of the dead Indian's skiff as an enormously predictive image of the future course of Peter Matthiessen's life: "He felt at peace, his effort displacing thought, the strokes of the oars building a harmony with the ocean rhythm, the vast invisible world where man had come from and which Daniel Barleyfield had gone back to, he crawling naked across its sunwarmed surface, so cold and still beneath, like a fly across a great dark carcass parching on a strand" (RR, 284). George McConville, like other young heroes of American literature, Natty Bumppo, Henry

David Thoreau (as character, not as author), Huck Finn, and Ike McCaslin, must divest himself before he can build a harmony with nature and confront the vast invisible world. Peter Matthiessen, in his own life, would undergo successive divestitures of wealth and civilization in the course of his experiences in the natural world, giving up the cosmopolitan sophistication of Paris in returning to the simple life of a Long Island fisherman, thereafter leaving wife and family to explore the American wilderness, and subsequently embracing the austere tenets of Zen Buddhism.

Partisans   *Partisans* (1955) is a novel *noir*, set in Paris, its back streets, and seamier underbelly. It is peopled with Communist Party members, street people, and an idealistic American journalist, who is impelled by an adolescent encounter with a Marxist guerrilla to seek him out, years later, ostensibly for an interview. Barney Sand, the journalist, is the rich young man of *Partisans*; his quest for Jacobi, the guerrilla, takes on the thematic overtones of a quest for meaningful action in life. The novel explores the need for political commitment in the face of poverty and injustice, but it also expands into questions about the methodology and efficacy of such action, scrutinizing the Marxist response and finding it lacking.

As in *Race Rock*, the terms of the ideological search are framed by two important figures in the protagonist's life: his father, a patriotic American diplomat, and Jacobi, a loyal Communist revolutionary. Barney Sand has had all of the benefits of his father's position and wealth in his upbringing, just like George McConville in *Race Rock*. But partly because of this upbringing, which involved considerable travel, Barney was exposed to other sides of life, including a chance meeting with the Marxist guerrilla, Jacobi, when Barney was fourteen and the family was fleeing Spain in 1938. It is a meeting Barney can never forget, for the laconic, resourceful Jacobi not only helps them escape, but seems to possess himself and his purpose in life like no one the young Barney has met. Barney's father resents the impression Jacobi has made upon his son, and the two men stand over the boy, poised in a brief scene of opposition that figures the rest of the book: "In the long moment that the two men stood gauging each other Barney remained seated between them, enthralled. His father's hand still rested on his shoulder, but Jacobi's hand lay lightly on Barney's wineglass, as if to protect this symbol of their friendship from Consul Sand."[4]

And so, years later, on assignment from his American magazine, Barney takes the opportunity to find Jacobi and interview him. The process, however, is not easy, for Jacobi has outlived his usefulness to the Party, is seen by them as a threat because of his knowledge, and is under Party custody. The search involves intermediaries, who themselves become emblems of different political stances, and a series of experiences that expose Barney to the realities of urban poverty and degradation. It is in the light of these experiences, his dialogue with intermediaries, and finally his meeting with Jacobi that Barney directs his idealism, and the novel resolves the question of the rich young man: What shall I do with my life to make it count?

The initial line of Barney's questioning of the American way is spurred by the early meeting with Jacobi, whose words sharpen the terms of the ideological conflict: "Your father and people like him represent the few. These few control the money and the churches and the armies, and they are powerful. . . . But we represent the many . . . and we are going to win" (*P*, 27). Jacobi's words stay with Barney, and Barney's father feels compelled to offset the Communist's influence on his son's thinking. Mr. Sand admits that Jacobi may be well-intentioned and therefore patriotic but "he is in the wrong, and history will judge him accordingly" (*P*, 59). And, while Barney is inclined to agree with his father based on his experiences in Czechoslovakia, he embarks on his quest "determined . . . to see Jacobi before repudiating the man's cause" (*P*, 66).

Barney meets a succession of people before he finds Jacobi. Rudi Gleize, as sleazy as his name and Barney's contact to the political underworld, leads him to Lise and Oliver, former Party members, who lead him to an important Party spokesman, Marat. The latter emerges as a major voice of Communist theory in the novel, as he takes Sand on a personal tour of Paris's lower depths. The sights and smells of poverty, along with Marat's constant indoctrination, have their effect on Barney, who finally wonders "if the harsh cures of the Party were not indeed, the sole solution" (*P*, 130). Before he reaches Jacobi, Barney has come to accept the Party's rationale that "the world is in need of change," but he remains at arm's distance from personal involvement, for he resents the way Jacobi, the faithful servant of Party policy, is being treated. Jacobi's purging represents the domination of theory over virtue for Barney.

The long-awaited meeting between Barney and Jacobi is orchestrated by Marat with the intention of discrediting Jacobi, who will be fingered as a collaborator with an American espionage agent, Barney. Although he cares little for his own reputation and remains loyal to the Party's objectives, Jacobi repudiates the Party's methods. In response to Barney's search for meaningful action, Jacobi advises him to return to America and help reform the system from within.

The final movement of the novel, developing Jacobi's advice and Barney's experience of how the Party treats its loyal hero, leads Barney to a firm rejection of Marxism and a return to government service in America. Ultimately he realizes that his father and Jacobi are not really opposites after all. In fact, when his father gets into trouble with the foreign service over failing to report an encounter with Jacobi, Barney sees a similarity in the two faithful servants who are ill-treated by the larger organizations they have obeyed. He envisions "his father's face, the cool, humorous, dedicated eyes; and these eyes merged with those of Jacobi . . . of every man at bay before himself" (*P,* 180).

Partisans, like *Race Rock,* resolves the clash of opposites by means of a synthesis. This time it is a synthesis of two opposing ideological positions, American diplomat versus Communist partisan, through the personal virtues of both men. Effectively the novel opts for individual virtue rather than ideological solutions with Barney's realization that "their causes . . . seemed remote and unimportant" (*P,* 182). Ultimately Barney acts out of personal, rather than global, altruism, trying to help Jacobi by promising Marat he will not publish the story of what happened as long as Jacobi remains unharmed. He also returns to America, intent on helping his father clear his name.

The book's resolution, while positive, is not cavalier. It espouses an optimism of *effort,* tempered by the bleak vision of poverty Barney has witnessed. The only answer offered is that of struggle: "Yet he had to try again, tomorrow in America; he had to keep on trying. And perhaps that trying would come to something in the end, though he might never see the sense in it" (*P,* 183). Two images close the book. The first is of a dirty streetcleaner, who with his cigarette pops the balloon of an Arab child, uttering a racist epithet, "*Va-t'en, negrillon.*" Barney, who is watching, meets the streetcleaner's drunken stare with sad understanding, "Yes, I know you, Barney thought, I'm not angry with you" (*P,* 184). The final image is of Barney failing to stop a taxi in the morning rush hour. The cabs are "caught in the heedless sweep of cars, big blind black cars of couriers of world affairs" (*P,* 184). The two images represent Matthiessen's sober vision of the obstacles to progress: the individual act of cruelty impelled by a cycle of poverty and racism, and the impersonal, blind forces of modern bureaucracy.

The idea for the *Partisans* was conceived in Paris, and the exciting intellectual mix and bizarre geographical atmosphere of Paris energize the novel. Written in the early fifties, *Partisans* reflects a time more given to political and personal idealism than today. The book also reflects the realities of the cold war and the shadow of McCarthyism in America. One can see the imprint of these forces on a young man like Matthiessen, painfully aware of the privileged beneficence of his education and upbringing and now determined to make his independent way. The ending of *Race Rock* has its young protagonist leaving home in vision of new horizons, a move paralleling Matthiessen's settling in Paris. The ending of *Partisans* has its counterpart heading back to America, a move mirroring Matthiessen's return to Long Island in 1953, one motivated by the same kind of personal ideals as those of Barney Sand.

Raditzer   *Raditzer* (1961) is a short, controlled, artistically finished novel, reminiscent in its themes and sea setting of Conrad's "The Secret Sharer." Charlie Stark is the central consciousness in whom the events of the novel are registered. Like his counterparts in Matthiessen's first two novels, Stark is both young and well-off. At twenty-six he enlists in the navy despite opportunities either to serve as an officer or to avoid the war altogether. He befriends Jack Gioncarlo and is immediately befriended himself by Raditzer, a ratlike opportunist who attaches himself to Stark because of Stark's ideals, which are clearly above the ordinary and which amaze and puzzle Raditzer. Stark tolerates the connection, arguing with Gioncarlo about Raditzer's essential humanity, but Stark ultimately is alone in his openness to Raditzer, "sharp-eyed and quick-fingered, a sort of human magpie."[5]

The novel is again about the growth of a rich young man through a choice that is thrust upon him. Instead of being faced with alternative figures calling upon his allegiance, however, as in the first two novels, here he must accept or reject a single individual and all that he represents. That individual is Raditzer, and he is everything that Charlie Stark is not. He is the outcast and the savage, while Charlie is the central and civilized man. The values that hang in the balance of Charlie Stark's judgment are familiar from *Race Rock* and *Partisans*: privilege or deprivation, civilization or savagery. However, the emphasis in *Raditzer* has shifted from the need to deal with one's own inheritance and one's own vocation to the necessity of confronting the totally other in society and in oneself.

There is no question of the difference between Raditzer and Stark. The former is an orphan, whose only name on his birth certificate was "Male Raditzer." He has "never had a family or even an address, referring instead to the bars, brothels, and all-night diners of towns up and down the coast as if these well-lit places had been home to him at night. . . "(*R*, 40). Raditzer is an uneducated and unloved drifter, used to surviving by his guile, street smarts, and irrepressibility. His wedge-shaped head and large, cocked ears give him a rodent-like appearance. He is cynical about humanity, profane in his language, and tactless in dealing with others. Stark, on the other hand, is the child of grace, with doting parents, a college education, and a lovely wife. While his father expects him to eventually become a lawyer and take over his firm, Charlie is also sensitive and artistic, settling ambiguously on a double major of art and pre-law. Most important, Charlie is an idealist, refusing his parents' offers of a custom-made life, going out of his way to serve his country in the latter stages of World War II by having a knee operation that enables him to enlist, and setting himself apart from the other enlisted men by his kindness to Raditzer and his faithfulness to his wife.

There are two thematic levels in Stark's decision to accept Raditzer's overtures of friendship while all the other men on board the *U.S.S. General Pendleton*, including Gioncarlo, ostracize him. The first and simplest has to do with sympathy for the underprivileged. Charlie Stark doesn't like Raditzer any more than the others do. In fact, Raditzer seems essentially unlikable. Yet Stark looks at Raditzer with the same understanding with which Barney Sand looked at the dirty streetcleaner who popped the child's balloon in *Partisans*. He accepts Raditzer because he is a human being and he has suffered. Stark tells Gioncarlo that there are only two choices in dealing with someone like Raditzer. "One choice is to tolerate him, on the grounds that he shares the human condition—"; and Gioncarlo interrupts with the second, "And the other is . . . kill him, on the grounds that he don't" (*R*, 112). Charlie makes the first choice, and he is rewarded with a deeper insight into himself as a result.

What Charlie finds out is that his concept of Raditzer's essential humanity involves more than he thought. He at first believes that Raditzer is human in spite of his aberrance. He subsequently learns that Raditzer's aberrance is a fundamental part of humanity. Raditzer represents the crippled nature of humanity, a moral ugliness that Charlie comes to realize he also shares. Matthiessen's implication is that, as the man of civilization confronts and accepts the outcast in society, he gradually discovers the beast within himself.

At first Charlie is pleased with himself in his lone acceptance of Raditzer, self-consciously proud of his liberal, humanistic attitude, a product of what Raditzer calls "no-bless oblige" (*R*, 35). Raditzer refuses to allow Charlie to operate on that plane, however, testing and tempting Charlie until he yields to the sexual charms of Myrna. But instead of being happy at Charlie's fall from grace, Raditzer is crushed; for, despite the testing, Charlie's integrity represented the possibility of virtue in a world of vice. When Raditzer sees the guilty and drunken Charlie at the bottom of a trench, we cannot help but recall the opening scene when Raditzer was in the ship's hole and Charlie pulled him out. Now the tables have been turned, and the impotent

Raditzer is not able to do the same thing for Charlie. Drawn low into Raditzer's world of sexual infidelity, Charlie falls even further when Raditzer provokes him to violent feelings by sending a letter to Charlie's wife informing her of her husband's sexual betrayal. Charlie diminishes in stature even more as he openly expresses his hatred for Raditzer: "You come near me or my wife ever again, and I'll kill you myself" (R, 142).

Yet Raditzer's effect on Charlie is ultimately beneficial, for it makes Charlie live in the real world of his own savagery, even admitting to himself that he liked hitting Raditzer, although the blow was delivered to save the latter's life. Raditzer is an even stronger shadow for Charlie Stark than Cady was for George McConville, compelling Charlie to face what he "would not face, a secret self, a specter escaped from the dark attic of the mind. He was the bogeyman in childhood cellars . . . but he was also the wretched troll within, the practitioner of dirty adolescent habits, the latent liar, pervert, coward, suddenly incarnate" (R, 43).

As in his first two novels, Matthiessen resolves the story's dilemma by means of synthesis. Charlie Stark becomes whole only by accepting Raditzer. Civilization can grow only if it realizes its own savagery. At the end, Charlie knows both himself and Raditzer better. Because he has faced his hatred, Charlie is more attached to Raditzer, for he sees their common humanity now in the context of their common evil. He may be a sadder person, but it is the sadness of experience. All along Raditzer said, "I know you, Charlie," and he was instrumental in Charlie's growth in self-knowledge, about his loveless marriage, about his frailty, about his shadow. Symbolically, Charlie recognizes this debt when the officer asks who knows the man missing from roll call and Charlie steps forward, claiming "I know him" (R, 146). After Raditzer falls to his death, Charlie is a deeper and better person for his admission of his own and others' responsibility. There are not two worlds, the civilized and the savage, Matthiessen implies, but one. And the man of civilization must take responsibility for his savagery.

Early Accomplishment and Promise

None of the three early novels won any prizes. The reviewers, with their characteristic generosity toward first novels, liked *Race Rock* best. Maurice Cranston, writing in the *London Magazine*, said the novel's "passion and pessimism, its moral guts and psychological knowledge, its eloquence and its humanity put it closer, if to anyone, to Conrad. . . . I know of no American novelist of his age or less who has written anything so good as this."[6] *Partisans* was treated more harshly, a fate frequently allotted to the successor of a successful debut. In the *New York Times Book Review* William Goyen called the characters "only mouthpieces. They are not empowered by depth of dramatic conviction. . . ."[7] Like other reviewers, James Finn praised Matthiessen for "taking serious risks," but damned the result as "a novel of ideas that does not quite come off."[8] And *Raditzer* was evaluated somewhere between the two, only closer to the first book. Granville Hicks lauded Matthiessen's "ability to give new life to an old theme," and felt the book was "important."[9] The *New Yorker* criticized the novel for deteriorating, after a strong beginning, "into a singularly unimpressive climax," but it credited Matthiessen with "a clear, pointed style, . . . a sense of atmosphere and the ability to communicate it."[10] My own opinion is that each book improves on its predecessor, a progression that would continue with Matthiessen's subsequent two novels.

Race Rock is a novel of youth in more ways than one. It suffers from overwriting, an exuberance of metaphor that occasionally becomes mixed, and an excessive anthropomorphizing of nature, all three qualities exemplified (excepting the mixed metaphor) in the following sentence: "On the headstone the wind laid a hand of rampant grass whose pettish fingers, scraping across the dates, pointed up the peculiarity of this moment, the feeling he had that now, in this very hour, he was leaving youth in favor of maturity" (*RR*, 5). The book also lacks control in its point of view, the center of consciousness passing among all four of the major characters and even to some minor ones. Another sign of the novel's immaturity is its taking the posturing of its principal characters too seriously. The earnestness of George McConville characterizes the 1950s as much as Jay McInerney's protagonist in *Bright Lights, Big City* typifies the facile hipness of the 1980s; in both cases the authors needed more distance from their main characters in order to maintain perspective. On the other hand, except for its occasional excesses, the writing in *Race Rock* is solid throughout. The setting is evocative, and the handling of flashbacks and present time is smooth and effective. The book's major virtue is its ability to dramatize its concerns in vivid and memorable scenes, especially the pivotal childhood scene of Percy Shipman's cat and the climactic weekend at Shipman's Point. On the whole, it is the perfect first novel, good enough to encourage its author by its recognizable merits, but not so good as to create an impossible standard to match in future endeavors, which is what happened with another first novel in the early 1950s, J. D. Salinger's *Catcher in the Rye.*

Given its theme of youthful search for ideals, *Partisans* might have easily been done poorly. In fact, the resolution of the novel's quest is a bit facile and open-ended considering the previous degree of ideological anguish undergone by its protagonist, Barney Sand. Yet Matthiessen has curbed the excesses of *Race Rock* with spare, careful writing; and the book treats serious political and intellectual issues judiciously. The book has style, convincing dialogue and a fine architectonic balance, beginning in light, slipping into the darkness of the Parisian underground, and emerging into light. And this physical movement parallels the intellectual evolution of its central character. It feels like the 1950s in a *cinema noir* way, creating a desperate, fatalistic atmosphere as its protagonist gets caught up in something bigger than himself, wondering about his search, "if he had ever controlled it at all, or if he had only been controlled by it. He felt himself a prisoner, not of the bookshop, nor even of Marat, but of himself, of some fatuous diehard hope of man" (*P*, 115). Sand is like those early detectives in American fiction, Chandler's Marlow for example, who have a firm conscience in personal loyalties and a dogged courage in pursuit of goals. Because he is easy to identify with and because his quest retains its air of danger and mystery, the ideological discussions, which some reviewers criticized, are quite palatable. Perhaps the charge that Matthiessen's characters seem more spokesmen than individuals can be explained by the book's spareness. It does concentrate more on atmosphere than character, but this, I submit, is more virtue than fault. The city of Paris, with its beauty and its poverty, takes on a life of its own: "The swirling night, refracting the city lights, was misty purple, like bad amethyst. He turned to the right and around the block, as directed, and went on walking. This was a market area, shuttered in iron. There were grilles on the shop windows, and heavy padlocks on the grilles. *Clip,clap, clip, clap*, rang his heels, the sound imprisoned in the street" (*P*, 119). On the whole, *Partisans* is a tighter, more daring, and better novel than Matthiessen's more highly esteemed debut.

Raditzer, however, is the most successful of the three early books because of the vivid characterization of its unlikable namesake, greater stylistic control than *Race Rock*, a less clichéd ending than *Partisans*, and a less dated quality than either of the two previous novels. The character of Raditzer deserves to go down in the petty knaves' Hall of Fame, although Matthiessen communicates not only his rascality but, what really distinguishes the portrait, his essential innocence. No scene illustrates this combination better than when Raditzer is disillusioned by the very infidelity he had been pressing on his friend Charlie Stark. When Stark exclaims, "Well, isn't that what you've been trying for three damned months to get me to do?" Raditzer rejoins, "No, I ain't. . . . Christ, I thought you was different, I thought at least you and Charlotte—" (*R*, 95). Ultimately Raditzer plays the role of Charon, ferrying the self-righteous Charlie to a confrontation with his own devils, but all the while hoping that Charlie would resist the journey. In the end, the trip with Raditzer paradoxically saves Charlie Stark, for Charlie grows in self-knowledge and finds the essential human connection between the alienating Raditzer and himself. Like Melville in "Bartleby, the Scrivener," Matthiessen displays the potentially salvific effect of the intrusion of the unpleasant upon the ordinary. The theme of the book is less far-reaching than those of its predecessors, but perhaps this is what allowed the author greater control. Within its limited scope, *Raditzer* is a fine novel, one that exhibits Matthiessen's ability to imagine himself into an alien persona, a quality that would serve him well in his subsequent nonfiction explorations.

One thing that is clear from the start of Peter Matthiessen's fictional career is his way with words. His voice, from the outset, is confident: evocative in descriptions of nature, spare and clean in setting scenes, and believable in dialogue. Except for the typical overwriting of youthful exuberance in some of his depictions of nature, nothing linguistic gives Matthiessen away as a novice in his first novels. He had won the *Atlantic Monthly* Prize for fiction with his story "Sadie," written while he was still in college; his style in these first novels has the finish of good short-story writing. Here is a typical passage from *Race Rock*: "The early sun of autumn Saturday was heatless on old hands, lumped and clumsy on his thighs like rusted tools. And he thought, my time is coming, all right, and he thought of how at Abraham's death so long ago the village heads were shaken over him for the last time, a thousand odd of them bobbing and turning and swaying back and forth like so many glass balls strung on a gill net in the sea, heads that today were underground, most of them, in pieces like old white clam shells" (*RR*, 23). This is polished writing, the metaphors carefully taken from the local trades of carpentry and fishing, the rhythms and sounds appropriately sonorous. Even in the light of Matthiessen's long and successful writing career, not one of his first novels is an embarrassment. They are daring ventures, artistically crafted; and, while none of them is an achievement of major proportions, each is interesting, insightful, and indicative of what was to come.

Chapter Three

Native Son and Naturalist: The Urge to Observe

Wildlife in America, The Shorebirds of North America

When Peter Matthiessen jumped into his old Ford convertible in late 1956 and set out to "explore the territory" of the United States Wildlife Refuges, he was Natty Bumppo sauntering into the wilderness, Rip Van Winkle scrambling up one of the highest parts of the Catskill Mountains, and young Henry David Thoreau sliding his canoe into the Concord River. Matthiessen was leaving behind a marriage of four years' duration because, as he explains it, "I needed to get the wandering out of my system that I hadn't done before I got married" (personal interview). He was relinquishing home, family, and society for a solitary journey into the West, the unknown, mirroring the movement away from conventional paths that runs throughout the central texts of American literature: Hester Prynne's venture into the forest at night, Ahab's wild pursuit of the great white whale, Huck Finn's push off from civilization on the raft of freedom. In his earlier move to Paris, Matthiessen had followed the other unconventional direction, the transatlantic voyage to our European past, forged by such equally central American predecessors as Henry James, T. S. Eliot, and Ernest Hemingway. In returning to America in 1953 and thereafter setting out to explore its remaining wilderness areas, Matthiessen was obeying the insistent command of Emerson to the American writer to "build your own world," to experience nature firsthand and make that experience the subject matter of his writing, to rely upon the "essence of genius, of virtue, and of life, which we call Spontaneity or Instinct."[1]

At Yale Matthiessen had read and liked Emerson and Thoreau, although he remembers no overwhelming sense of allegiance or any conscious following of the precepts of the American Transcendentalists. Yet the legacy of Emerson and Thoreau is there throughout his career, and Emerson's description of the Poet perfectly describes the young Matthiessen embarking upon his trip west: "He had left his work and gone rambling none knew whither, and had written hundreds of lines, but could not tell whether that which was in him was therein told; he could tell nothing but that all was changed—man, beast, heaven, earth and sea."[2] Emerson's essay "The Poet," in fact, is a veritable blueprint of the whole enterprise of Matthiessen's first nature books. According to Emerson, the Poet's initial impulse comes from direct experience, something he has in common with all men. On most of us, however, "too feeble fall the impressions of nature . . . to make us artists. Every touch should thrill." The Poet, on the other hand, "sees and handles that which others dream of, traverses the whole scale of experience, and is representative of man, in virtue of being the largest power to receive and to impart" ("The Poet," 219). His inspiration is from Nature which "offers all her creatures to him as a picture-language" of the ineffable. His word must be "the truest," and his phrase "the fittest, most musical." But Emerson insists it is not simply skill with language that makes this utterance musical, but rather "a thought so passionate and alive that like the spirit of a plant or an animal it has an architecture of its own, and adorns nature with a new thing" ("The Poet," 221).

Each of these characteristics applies to the young Matthiessen as he gathers together the impressions of a few months' experiences in the American wildlife refuges into his first book of nonfiction, *Wildlife in America* (1959, rev. ed. 1987). The influence cannot have been entirely unconscious, for Matthiessen makes reference to Emerson's philosophic view of nature in the book, although he makes no mention of Emerson's view of the Poet, which would have indeed been out of place. Matthiessen would never claim the mantle of Emerson's Poet for himself, as Walt Whitman did, for he finds such self-assertion inherently distasteful and ultimately irrelevant to his work. The unity of Matthiessen's whole opus of fiction and nonfiction is understandable, however, when we see its author standing in the direct shadow of Emerson's Poet. Immediate experience, remarkable powers of observation, scrupulous accuracy, inspiration from nature, and passionate verbal power characterize the core of Peter Matthiessen's literary enterprise. Even his novels draw upon the immediacy of his own experiences, the two most successful of them, *At Play in the Fields of the Lord* and *Far Tortuga,* drawn directly from personal adventures described by the author in separate, factual accounts. Of course, in his typical works of nonfiction, Matthiessen travels to an area like the Peruvian jungle or an island in the Bering Strait and lives there for a time, maintaining a daily journal, until he is able to later retire to his writing desk. His manuscripts are routinely submitted to the thorough scrutiny of experts in the various disciplines bearing upon his explorations (naturalists, anthropologists, ornithologists, etc.) in order to insure their accuracy. As for nature, it is everywhere in his writing, his commitment and passion for it nowhere more vividly shown than in his first book of nonfiction on the changing picture of American wildlife and in his subsequent account of the shorebirds of North America.

These two books clearly exhibit Matthiessen as integral to the American literary tradition of Emerson and Thoreau: Emerson, the theorist of the vocation, and Thoreau, its practitioner. Firsthand experience, self-reliance, immersion in nature, transition to a new state, and truth telling are among the major values propounded by Emerson in his essays and practiced by Thoreau in both his journeys around Concord and his accounts of the same. These same virtues are the essence of Matthiessen's trip across America in 1956–58, his lifelong observations of shorebirds, and the two books that resulted. Of course, like his two 19th-century predecessors who graduated from Harvard, Matthiessen practices an informed experience, also based upon an ivy education (Matthiessen's at Yale) with its attendant respect for scholarship. One should remember that Emerson's essays about the importance of the here and now are strewn with allusions and citations from the past, building his famous essay "Nature," for example, on the scholastic distinction between passive and active nature, *natura naturata* and *natura naturans*.[3]

So also, Matthiessen's books on wildlife are grounded solidly on the work of previous naturalists. His research is painstaking, with generous citations from those who have preceded him in observing the creatures of the wild and in reporting their histories, habits, and encounters with man. When the books are anecdotal, they narrate stories of the species themselves, not of Matthiessen's adventures in the wild. His firsthand experience, however, grounds the accounts, resulting in an assurance, immediacy, and authenticity of narrative voice. For example, when the author presents a picture of prairie life as it was interrupted by the advent of man, one senses that his imaginative scene is grounded in close observation of the same animals today:

[T]he mule deer, elk, and pronghorn antelope, in company with the bison, only lifted their heads to view the pack trains and covered wagons and the strange, broad-hatted, upright figures on the horses' backs. Alert, at a little distance, they would stand stock still in the high grasses, tails flicking, jaws working, not as yet alarmed. But soon they learned to move away, the bison heaving into their ponderous, dusty canter, the antelope scampering, tail patches flashing white, the elk and deer pausing in their dignified, neat-footed flight to stare back, round-eyed, at the intruders.[4]

Matthiessen's firsthand experience extends to interviews with those who live among the creatures of the wild—game wardens, park rangers, and others—providing information not otherwise available.

One must remember that up to this point in his career, Matthiessen had published two novels and a few short stories, and had founded a strictly literary journal. Returning to Long Island to do commercial fishing in 1954 had represented a radical recasting of his personal life, shaped heretofore by a strictly literary and cosmopolitan mold. Leaving home and family for the American wilderness, of course, was another radical personal transition, and the consequent expenditure of enormous energy in research and observation in the service of a factual chronicle of American wildlife marked an equally major transition in his writing career. It is true that he had always been interested in nature and its creatures as a child, and he had taken courses in zoology and ornithology at Yale. However, to turn the concentration of his writing from short stories in the *Atlantic* and novels about youthful struggles and ambitions to detailed and exhaustive accounts of the creatures of the wild was a shift of immense proportions.

In retrospect, of course, it is apparent that movement is as much a part of Matthiessen's nature and the course of his life as it is of the shorebirds to whom he lovingly devotes an entire book. Movement had also been a major metaphor in Emerson, who said in "Self-Reliance," "Power ceases in the instant of repose; it resides in the moment of transition from a past to a new state, in the shooting of the gulf, in the darting to an aim" ("Self-Reliance," 42). Emerson's remark could serve as a gloss on Matthiessen's career, which has involved continual "transition from a past to a new state" in matters of location, type of writing, personal relationship, and spiritual vision. Matthiessen's life has been so essentially nomadic that it led to the breakup of his first marriage and put considerable strain on his second. He admitted to me that he is "hard on women," because of the time he consumes in travel and writing. Although in the last few years he has spent greater periods of time at home, this is only a stability relative to the long and frequent trips of the 1960s and 1970s. At the time of my visit to Sagaponack in August 1989, Matthiessen was planning a trip west in search of grizzly bears; and, when I spoke with him in January 1990, he was readying to go to Russia.[5] His beloved wind birds, who fly at the high altitudes suited to their globe-spanning propensities, symbolize Matthiessen's essentially migratory soul.

In *Wildlife in America* Matthiessen gives credit to Emerson and Thoreau as being among the literary figures of the American past who "watered the seeds of what would become known as conservation" (*WA*, 140). He also praises Francis Parkman, who journeyed west in 1846 and described his exploits in *The Oregon Trail* (1849). Parkman, we are told, not only did much to awaken the curiosity of Easterners about the natural beauty and riches of the American West, he also exhibited a passionate interest in the Indian tribes. Indeed Parkman is Matthiessen's predecessor in more ways than one. Parkman had also been young, only twenty-three, and well educated, a Harvard graduate, when he blazed the western trail into unknown territories. The young explorer's day-to-day journal became the basis of his narrative of events, interlaced with description and reflection, providing a model that Matthiessen would follow, not so much in his early wildlife books, but in many subsequent travel accounts like *The Cloud Forest, The Tree Where Man Was Born,* and *Oomingmak*. And Parkman's then unique observations of the Oglala Indians, with reports of their conversation and way of life, would be imitated by Matthiessen among the 20th-century Oglalas and other tribes in his *Indian Country*. Even Parkman's tone in his Preface to the 1892 edition of *The Oregon Trail* anticipates the nostalgic lament of Matthiessen's naturalist and Indian books over the extinction of wild animals and the disruption of the old ways. Parkman wrote:

The buffalo is gone, and of all his millions nothing is left but bones. Tame cattle and fences of barbed wire have supplanted his vast herds and boundless grazing grounds. Those discordant serenaders, the wolves that howled at evening about the traveller's camp-fire, have succumbed to arsenic and hushed their savage music. The wild Indian is turned into an ugly caricature of his conqueror; and that which made him romantic, terrible, and hateful, is in large measure scourged out of him. The slow cavalcade of horsemen armed to the teeth has disappeared before parlor cars and the effeminate comforts of modern travel.[6]

Matthiessen seems to be acknowledging the exemplary influence of this predecessor in *Wildlife in America* by quoting liberally from his "vivid account of a frontier where 'curlew flew screaming over our heads, and a host of little prairie-dogs sat yelping at us at the mouths of their burrows on the dry plain beyond.'" (*WA,* 139–40).

Wildlife in America and *The Wind Birds,* in fact, are debts to all those American naturalists and literary figures who have toiled or written on behalf of wildlife. Matthiessen gives them all credit: "Audubon had not been the first naturalist to describe the frontier; Thomas Say, Titian Peale, Thomas Nuttall, and John Townsend, among others, had preceded him. Nor was Parkman the first literary figure; his prominence derives not only from his narrative ability but from the fact that he wrote out of thorough experience" (*WA*, 140). Matthiessen mentions James Fenimore Cooper, who wrote of the West from his experience of the "eastern wilderness and eastern Indian," and Washington Irving, whose *Tour of the Prairies* was based upon an excursion of only two weeks. Despite the limitations of their experiences, however, the two are credited with "much of the contemporary public interest in wildlife and the natural resources of the nation, as well as the first significant warnings that these benefits were far from inexhaustible" (*WA*, 140). In his own two explorations of nature, with a decidedly esthetic bent, Matthiessen takes his place in this tradition of enlightened literary concern.

Wildlife in America

Matthiessen's history of American wildlife, with drawings by Bob Hines, is a lavish book, at once a paean to the beauty and majesty of the wild, an acknowledgment of all those who have spoken or acted on behalf of wild creatures, and a warning that the already significant losses of species will continue unless mankind changes its ways. The book is filled with details about individual species, especially those that have become extinct or imperiled by the encroachments of mankind. Many of the stories are sad, such as the extinction of the great auk. Astoundingly, the killing of the last pair of these birds was actually witnessed in early June 1844, off the coast of Iceland. Matthiessen begins the book with the great auk, "the first species native to North America to become extinct by the hand of man" (*WA*, 21), and its fate sets the pattern and tone for the rest of the book. The gray wolf, the black-footed ferret, the whooping crane, the cougar, the buffalo, the Bachman's warbler, the jaguar, and the passenger pigeon are some of the characters in this history, most of them deplorably extirpated or endangered on our continent.

Appearing as it did in 1959, three years before Rachel Carson's popular *Silent Spring, Wildlife in America* has had an impact on the subsequent environmental awakening and conservation movement. The book was enthusiastically received by reviewers when it first appeared. Edward Weeks called it "the first modern and comprehensive record of our wildlife,"[7] and Rae Brooks hailed it as a "wonderful book" written "with grace and sureness always."[8] Archie Carr in the *New York Times Book Review* said: "This is a dramatic, unsettling story, skillfully told in a clean, strong prose not often found in the literature of conservation. The author never veers toward either sentimentality or over-documentation. . . . If his book is as widely read as it deserves to be, our descendants may be much in debt to Peter Matthiessen."[9] Given such a reception, it is not surprising that the book continues in print today in a revised edition that has been brought up to date with new information assembled by Michael Bean, who contributed the bulk of the new epilogue. Although *Wilderness* magazine criticized the new edition because "too much of the text still documents thirty-year-old assumptions, not all of which have survived the wear–and–tear of the decades," it recognized the appendix's usefulness in correcting most of these assumptions and calls the book "one of the central texts in the history of wildlife in this country."[10]

Most of the recent news for endangered wildlife is not good. The black-footed ferret, which seemed to come back from extinction in 1981, once again was skirting the edge of existence in 1985. The Devil's Hole pupfish, threatened by decreasing water supply and the consequent loss of photosynthesizing sunlight, also appears close to extinction. On a larger level, however, Matthiessen is able to report that the conservation movement has come a long way since his first edition of *Wildlife,* as exemplified by the birdwing pearly mussel, an invertebrate species with "no apparent commercial, recreational, or esthetic value," on whose survival the Tennessee Valley Authority has spent $4 million and set aside another $7 million for the years to come (*WA,* 268). Unfortunately, despite the largess of this unusual example, and despite the overall raising of environmental consciousness, many species of wildlife still teeter on the edge of extinction. The epilogue recounts the recently threatened condition of the six species of coastal sea turtles, the plight of the Devil's Hole pupfish and the Colorado River squawfish, and many other recent examples of "an unprecedented impoverishment of the diversity of life" (*WA,* 279).

Unlike the occasionally irrational and hysterical voices of conservationists, Matthiessen's tone throughout is even and calm. Even when recounting the tragic story of man's persistent insensitivity and cruelty, Matthiessen lets the actions speak for themselves, which makes his account all the more persuasive and enlightening. Sometimes his understandable dismay breaks through, as when he laments the disappearance of the bison:

The bison herds were almost certainly the greatest animal congregations that ever existed on earth, and the greed and waste which accompanied their annihilation doubtless warrants some sort of superlative also. Nevertheless, their disappearance was inevitable. Once the settlers discovered the agricultural potential of the long-grass prairies, and the ranchers bred fat livestock on the short-grass plains farther west, the history of these humped, sullen beasts was over. We can take comfort, though not much pride, in the fact that two wild herds were saved, for it is quite likely that, had Yellowstone Park not been recently established at the time, the bison would now be confined on earth to Canada alone. (*WA*, 151)

One sometimes forgets, in the overwhelming tide of historical forces like the above mentioned discovery by the western settlers of the agricultural potential of the prairies, that individuals do exert some influence on the course of events. Matthiessen, to his credit, cites many examples of individuals who made a difference. One such, who as a young man observed firsthand the wanton destruction of bison, was Theodore Roosevelt, "an ardent amateur biologist and naturalist" (*WA*, 152), who had a hand in the establishment of our national park system and its protective legislation. Another individual who made a contribution, on a smaller and more direct level, was Buffalo Jones, "the plainsman who became, at Yellowstone, the first federal warden in the United States" (*WA*, 152). Matthiessen recounts Jones's daring accomplishment of tying up an adult grizzly, removing a tin can wedged in its paw, and freeing it again. On another occasion, "Jones lassoed by the hind foot a grizzly which had been molesting human habitations, suspended it from a stout limb, and thrashed it soundly with a bean pole before releasing it" (*WA*, 152).

Always Matthiessen is a teacher. At one point he informs us that the crocodile was not discovered in America until 1819 despite nearly three centuries of Spanish occupation of Florida (*WA*, 39). At another, he instructs us that the sole hoofed mammal indigenous to North America is the pronghorn antelope, all the others having come by way of the Bering Strait in prehistoric times (*WA*, 141). And, on a more provocative note, he explains that when we think of a species of wild animals retreating from a civilized area to one less civilized, we harbor a misconception; for a retreat is impossible when the less civilized habitat is already filled to capacity by the same species: "In other words, when one speaks of a species . . . 'retreating,' one really means that it has been exterminated in certain units of its range . . ." (*WA*, 36).

Matthiessen's steady accumulation of evidence and his fluid style—he brings the same care about language shown in his early novels to his wildlife chronicle—make the book at once convincing and enormously readable. Few nature writers are as meticulous about their prose as Matthiessen. As a consequence, we continually happen upon descriptions that capture and memorialize particular creatures of the wild. My own favorite is his picture of the grizzly bear: "Solitary, huge, the bears bring to life the barren, alpine tundra, the dwarf birch and willow thickets, and the gravel bars of the swift, gray glacier rivers. . . . No one who has ever seen a grizzly will dispute its title [monarch of the wild]; shambling, rooting, or frozen against a hillside, fur roughened by the wind, it stirs the heart. For many of us, the great grizzly will always represent a wild, legendary America somewhere to the north and west which we were born too late ever to see" (*WA*, 90).

Matthiessen is equally adept in summary as in description, capsulizing the problem under discussion with succinct insights. For example, after recording the damage done to innumerable fish species when the Welland Ship Canal was built, Matthiessen says: "Man, like the rat and the mosquito, can adapt himself to virtually all terrestrial climates, and less resourceful creatures have no choice but to make room for him during his stay on earth" (*WA*, 211). Such a comparison between man and two of the species he most detests is shocking, and Matthiessen follows up the shock by quoting British ornithologist James Fisher's even larger indictment: "Man is the filthiest animal that has ever trod the face of the earth. Man is ineradicably, utterly filthy. And every great nation in every part of the world has made a colossal mess as it has exploited its way through its own country" (*WA*, 212).

A large part of the effectiveness of *Wildlife* rests upon the thorough research that accompanies its observations. Quotations like Fisher's, citations from naturalists, and letters from historical figures such as Buffalo Bill Cody (a "professional meat hunter") are sprinkled throughout. One cannot but be impressed by the detail of Matthiessen's research. The appendices include a list of endangered species and a chronology of legislation affecting wildlife. In fact, the book is a debt to the knowledge that has been collected about the wilderness and a gift to all those who have labored on behalf of the wild. Matthiessen is generous in crediting those who have struggled on behalf of the creatures of the wild. He also pays a personal debt to his parents in the book's dedication, "For E. C. M. and E. A. M. with love and thanks," a gesture of reconciliation after their wounded feelings from reading his first two books, novels that dealt with conflicts between parents and children. The subject matter of *Wildlife* is, of course, itself a gift to Matthiessen's father, who for many years had been an officer of the National Audubon Society. In every sense, the book shows Matthiessen to be a native son. In returning to a strictly American subject matter, in journeying west into the American wilderness, and in writing from his own firsthand experience, Matthiessen proved himself in his first book of nonfiction to be a loyal son of his American literary predecessors.

The Shorebirds of North America, revised as The Wind Birds

While Matthiessen crossed the country in his research on *Wildlife in America,* for his next wildlife volume, *The Shorebirds of North America* (1967), he was able to rely largely on observations made on a stretch of Long Island beach only a short walk from his back door. This very spot was where I interviewed Matthiessen in early August of 1989, just after the first wave of shorebirds had passed through in their seasonal migrations and before the second wave would come along in early September. Sagaponack Pond is separated from the ocean only by a small lip of beach, seasonally overflowed. "It's a great place for birds," Matthiessen remarked, "one of the richest there is." In *Shorebirds* he explains: "To the margins and vicinity of Sagaponack Pond come more than half of the shorebird species of North America, not only because of the pond's location on the Atlantic flyway but because of the range of habitats in a small area."[11] It is a freshwater pond right at the ocean's edge, a perfect locale for migrating shorebirds, some of whom never go near the salt water and some of whom rarely leave it, while most of the more plentiful species cross habitat lines rather frequently. Matthiessen obviously loves the area and the birds equally. In fact, *Shorebirds,* or as he renamed the book in a revised and reduced 1973 edition, *The Wind Birds,* is a labor and testimony of love for these winged creatures.

Matthiessen's text is the same in both editions, except for minor revisions. *Shorebirds,* however, is a much more elaborate production, a coffee-table extravaganza with artwork by Robert Clem, color paintings of the most common shorebirds in their natural habitats and pencil drawings as well. It also includes an introduction by its general editor, Gardner D. Stout, and an appendix by Ralph S. Palmer of rather technical "species accounts" of the seventy-five species occurring on this continent. The book is massive and gorgeous. In the revised version, Matthiessen retains only his text, an expanded version of the bibliography, and the index. In place of the paintings and drawings by Clem, Matthiessen has substituted pen-and-ink drawings by Robert Gillmore, which are bolder, less ethereal, but no less effective than Clem's pencil sketches. The revision makes the book more manageable and affordable, and focuses attention on the text itself, whereas Clem's color paintings of the individual birds in *Shorebirds* invited considerable contemplation.

Shorebirds's critical reception had the same ecstatic ring as that given to

Wildlife in America. Walter Harding called it "magnificent. . . . A real treasure."[12] John Hay, writing in *Natural History,* said it is "one of the finest books of natural history I have ever seen, regardless of its qualities as an ornithological text, which are considerable."[13] One reviewer, R. M. Mengel, did have reservations about the book's ornithological virtues, for he said the text "abounds with small factual errors and conceptual near misses (occasionally the misses are wide) . . ."; but even Mengel granted that the book "is abundantly documented, and the author's opinions (not always sound) clearly labeled as such" and that Matthiessen "has performed a distinct service in popularizing some important matters."[14] Most of the reviewers had no such cavils. Peter Farb, author of at least a dozen nature books, wrote in *Saturday Review* that the book is "among the finest nature books ever to come off the presses in this country" and that it "will someday rank as an important document in natural history."[15]

It is no wonder that Matthiessen loves the wind birds, as he calls them, for they answer to an essential longing of his own soul, a desire to be one with the seasonal changes of the world, an impulse to movement and change. Matthiessen is conscious of the affinity, explaining it thus: "The restlessness of shorebirds, their kinship with the distance and swift seasons, the wistful signal of their voices down the long coastlines of the world make them, for me, the most affecting of wild creatures."[16] He then goes on to elaborate on the welcomeness of shorebirds to any world traveller to exotic locales, for they may be "the lone familiar note in a strange land" (*WB,* 16). In his own case, four of the species common to Sagaponack, the spotted and white-rumped sandpipers and the black-bellied and golden plovers, cheered him by their respective appearances when he was high up in the Andes, at the Straits of Magellan, among the cane fields of Hawaii, and along the Great Barrier Reef. Matthiessen is truly in awe of these wind birds, their feats of long-distance flight and navigation, their migratory instincts, their distinguishing characteristics, and their sheer beauty. In the instance of the sanderling—the common sandpiper of summer beaches—he reminds us of the miraculous in the commonplace: "We stand there heedless of an extraordinary accomplishment: the diminutive creature making way for us along the beaches of July may be returning from an annual spring voyage which took it from central Chile to nesting grounds in northeast Greenland, a distance of eight thousand miles" (*WB,* 16–17).

Shorebirds appear in practically every book Matthiessen has written. In fact, of all the wild creatures he observes in his travels around the world, they are the most frequently mentioned. This is because, for Matthiessen, the shorebird touches closely upon the central mystery of life itself and its complex, always changing, migratory nature. Normally, Matthiessen's nature writing concentrates on observation and information, but this winged creature draws the author into the kind of symbolic interpretation that Emerson believed was essential to an appreciation of nature. Emerson said that "nature is a symbol, in the whole, and in every part" ("The Poet," 224). And in *The Wind Birds*, Matthiessen writes: "One has only to consider the life force packed tight into that puff of feathers to lay the mind wide open to the mysteries—the order of things, the why and the beginning. As we contemplate that sanderling, there by the shining sea, one question leads inevitably to another, and all questions come full circle to the questioner, paused momentarily in his own journey under the sun and sky" (*WB*, 17).

It is this life force, so essential to man's own journey, that Matthiessen is tracking when he exhaustively details the varieties, habitats, distinguishing traits, mating and nesting habits, taxonomic differences, and migratory patterns of the wind birds. It is a life force that drives some of the birds to incredible navigational feats. One of the most amazing is the case of the shearwater, released in Venice, which negotiated a trans-European, east-west journey out of all migration patterns, to alight at its home nesting ledge on a sherry in the Irish Sea after only twelve and a half days. The same life force causes many of the shorebirds to climb nearly three miles above the earth into the rarefied air of their long-distance migrations. It propels some species to dive underwater and swim if pursued or wounded, and it spurs the dunlin to fly at speeds up to 110 m.p.h. In perhaps its most powerful manifestation, this life force has generated the remarkable resurrection from near extinction of many threatened species of shorebirds. Some cases are still in the balance, but even these have made miraculous appearances after they had been mourned and buried.

The eleven chapters of *The Wind Birds* are the work of a dedicated naturalist with the serious intent of contributing not only to our knowledge but to our appreciation of these creatures of the air. Because of this, Matthiessen organizes the book not by species—the typical treatment of birds—but according to different aspects of the birds' lives: survival, nourishment, physiology, habits of flight, migration routes, speciation, mating, nesting, methods of defense, and habitats. The book's ambling, appreciative manner is reinforced by evocative quotations at the head of each chapter from literary or naturalist sources. Typical is the citation from Thoreau's *Walden*: "Perhaps no one dreamed of Snipe an hour ago, the air seemed empty of such as they; but as soon as the dusk begins, so that a bird's flight is concealed, you hear this peculiar spirit-suggesting sound, now heard through and above the evening din of the village" (*WB*, 83).

By this layered treatment of the shorebirds, interspersed with literary appreciations and his own detailed observations, Matthiessen makes the birds at once more real and more representative. They are the scattering birds of our summer beaches, and they are also the graceful power of the life force itself. The book, in fact, ends on a note both realistic and symbolic. Traditionally, the curlew and golden plover have an innate sense of bad weather approaching, which they manifest differently: the curlew departing the area, the golden plover emitting a high sad whistle. Because of this, these birds became known as "harbingers of death." Matthiessen suggests that there is a poetic justice in the legend, for the plover carries intimations of our own mortality in the "wild melodies of their calls, in the breath of vast distance and bare regions that attends them. . . . Yet it is not the death sign that the curlews bring, but only the memory of life, of a high beauty passing swiftly, as the curlew passes, leaving us in solitude on an empty beach, with summer gone, and a wind blowing" (WB, 150). The image recalls Matthew Arnold's beach and Wallace Stevens's birds making their "ambiguous undulations" as they disappear into the dark. While the beach is deserted after the birds have passed, the image of their presence, to use another Stevens metaphor, "plays / On the clear viol of . . . memory, / And makes a constant sacrament of praise."[17]

Chapter Four

South American Adventurer: The Reportorial or the Fictive Impulse

The Cloud Forest, At Play in the Fields of the Lord

Nonfiction or Fiction

Peter Matthiessen has combined a life of writing and a life of adventure, his expeditions to such remote parts of the globe as the outbacks of New Guinea, the Himalayas, Africa's Serengeti plain, and the deepest Amazonian jungles largely financed by the *New Yorker,* which publishes his accounts of the trips. With a birder's eye, a botanist's knowledge, and an adventurer's soul, Matthiessen leads a host of contemporary travel writers in the best traditions of explorers like Burton and Stanley, Bruce and Shackleton, and naturalists like Thoreau and John Muir. Today's practitioners of the genre include the late Bruce Chatwin, Paul Theroux, Alex Shoumatoff, Edward Hoagland, Jeremy Bernstein, and Barry Lopez. As a group these writers discover the remote or the unusual and make it vicariously accessible to the ordinary reader. Matthiessen is in the minority, however, in that he is also a novelist of some regard, having written six novels, two of which, *Far Tortuga* (1975) and *At Play in the Fields of the Lord* (1965), have been quite well received.

So, why does a writer like Matthiessen or Chatwin, after one of his adventures, sometimes write fiction and sometimes nonfiction? For example, after his 1973 trip to the Himalayas with George Schaller in search of the elusive snow leopard, Matthiessen recounted the experience only in journal form, first in the *New Yorker,* then as the best-selling *The Snow Leopard* (1978). On the other hand, Matthiessen's 1967 turtling expedition out of Grand Cayman with a motley crew of fisherman was also paid for by the *New Yorker.* But when he came back, Matthiessen had to present the legendary editor William Shawn with his decision to withhold from his straightforward account of the trip ("To the Miskito Bank") "the best material" because there was something else he had to do with the experience; as he describes it, something bigger, more pressing, a novel. Matthiessen says he approached Shawn with some misgivings, expecting a rebuke or at least a financial demur. Instead, Shawn said at once, "Mr. Matthiessen, do what's best for the work." That work was published eight years later as *Far Tortuga* and praised for its daring experimentalism by reviewers, one of whom said it was "the most brilliant novel I have read about the sea since Joseph Conrad's *Nigger of the 'Narcissus.'*"[1]

The larger question, of course, is whence the impulse to write in one genre rather than the other. Why did Melville's sea voyages end up in novels? Why did Thoreau's meanderings on the Concord and Merrimac rivers and his experiment at Walden Pond result in nonfiction? Why did Hemingway's African safaris inspire both *The Green Hills of Africa* and two of his greatest short stories, "The Snows of Kilimanjaro" and "The Short Happy Life of Francis Macomber"? What better way to address the question of nonfictional versus fictional responses to experience than by examining an instance in which a writer produced both genres out of the same experience, a trip Matthiessen took in 1959–60 to the South American wilderness, again underwritten by the *New Yorker*. A straightforward account of the journey appeared first in the magazine and then the following year as *The Cloud Forest* (1961). Four years later came the novel, *At Play in the Fields of the Lord*. By observing how these books differ in their reflecting of the same experience, we may discover what it is about such experiences that triggers one response rather than the other. Perhaps this controlled attentiveness to two books from one experience can shed light on why Matthiessen never wrote a novel about his Himalayan adventure and why he withheld the "best material" from the report of his turtle-fishing venture for the *New Yorker*. My hope is that in the particular will be a paradigm of the general.

It is true that the boundary between fiction and nonfiction has been questioned in recent years. Practical discussion focuses on hybrid works like Capote's *In Cold Blood*, Wolfe's *Kandy-Kolored Tangerine Flake Streamline Baby*, and Mailer's *Armies of the Night*; critics see in these examples of the new journalism or nonfiction novel a form that "employs techniques drawn from the art of fiction to create something of fiction's atmosphere or feeling and that, more important, moves toward the intentions of fiction while remaining fully factual."[2] Yet whatever the specific definition of the hybrid genre, the very terms of the discussion (a blending of two separate forms) confirm the validity of the distinction between fiction and nonfiction. Indeed, the new journalism or the nonfiction novel paradoxically clarifies the boundary between fiction and nonfiction instead of clouding it, for in order to define what is new in these works, critics must rely on long-held assumptions about what is fiction and what is not. However diversely they describe the nonfiction novel's usurpation of fiction's intentions (e.g., "they have illuminated the ethical dilemmas of our time"[3]), critical discussion begins from a set of assumptions about what constitutes a fiction and what does not. In other words, the effort to identify a hybrid of nonfiction and fiction no more blurs the boundary between the two than the crossing of two breeds of dog casts doubt on the integrity of the separate breeds.

As in all good experiments, I begin with a simple hypothesis: Fictional narrative engages a part of the human psyche that nonfictional narrative leaves untouched. Or, to put it in terms of stimulus-response: the experience that evokes nonfictional narrative may awaken the observant eye, the inquiring mind, and perhaps even the sympathetic heart. It does not, however, awaken the blazing imagination. Impelled by its peculiar experience, then, nonfiction seeks to inform, share, chronicle, persuade, entertain, or excite to action. Fiction, fueled by a different *kind* of experience or the same experience differently felt, seeks to explain questions of human existence. "I will show you fear in a handful of dust." This line from Ecclesiastes, used by Eliot in "The Waste Land," encapsulates the enterprise of fiction. The novel does not simply use fear, it shows fear; that is, it helps us understand fear, or any fundamental human emotion, and it accomplishes this through the particles of existence, handfuls of the beginnings and endings of things ("From dust do you come, and unto dust you shall return"). Nonfiction tells us what happened and what was seen, thought, felt, but it does not show us significance, reverberation. It may employ fear, but it does not show fear, that is, reveal what fear is all about. Thus nonfictional narrative lacks a mythic dimension because it is not fueled by the need to explain existential human questions. At least, that was my initial hypothesis. Now on to the two books, their common experiential sources, and an attempt at empirical verification.

The Cloud Forest

The Cloud Forest (1961) is indeed straightforward reporting. It is subtitled "A Chronicle of the South American Wilderness," and at one place Matthiessen calls it a "journal of the mountains."[4] During the course of this journal, Matthiessen functions as an observer of and commentator on the natural world of South America's mountains, ruins, jungles, rivers, animals, insects, birds, fish, and people—including a multitude of Indian tribes and inhabitants of both short and long duration. The book covers five months of travel up, down, and across the continent by boat, plane, train, bus, car, canoe, raft, and foot. "This is an account of Matthiessen's pilgrimage," says one reviewer, "to the primeval . . . from the Amazon jungles, across the Andes, around the strange bare country of Tierra del Fuego, into the great frontierland of Mato Grosso, and through some of the wild, unmapped areas of Peru."[5] The narrative moves in an aimless, informative fashion, typical of the *New Yorker*'s travel pieces. Indeed, Matthiessen remarks at one point, "Through various causes, not the least of these some remarkably bad planning, I crossed the Andes nine times in five months, at various points from northern Peru to Tierra del Fuego" (*CF,* 68). During the course of these meanderings, the writer is certainly not timid in entertaining opinions about larger questions of South American society, politics, and religion, such as his condemnation of the creation of Brasilia, the Brazilian capitol, as "less inspired than pretentious, a brave new city cunningly disguised as a World's Fair" (*CF,* 117), or his sweeping indictment of South American bribery: "Money pretty much has its way throughout all of South America, to a degree quite startling even to a mind grown hardened to the spectacular graft and corruption in the United States" (*CF,* 122).

Matthiessen's primary interest in *The Cloud Forest,* however, is in place, atmosphere, natural phenomena, customs, and character, marshalling an impressive amount of information and observation, and delivering it fresh. Crossing, for example, the Sargasso Sea in November, he tells us that "all breeding adults of the common fresh-water eel of North America, North Africa, and Europe, arriving at unknown rates, by unknown routes, are now convening: by spring, myriad blade-shaped larvae will have hatched from eggs suspended in the murk one hundred fathoms down, and a year later (three years, in the case of the smaller European form) will enter the river mouths, ascend the streams, in the shape of elvers" to remain and grow until "after a period of five to twenty years these yellowish eels will change one autumn to a clean marine silver and, reversing the life process of the salmon, make their way back to the sea, to that vast backwater thousands of submarine miles away upon which now, by the hand of a mustachioed Brazilian seaman, we splash a great pail of nutrient garbage and pass on" (*CF,* 9–10). Matthiessen repeats the report by Colonel P. H. Fawcett, the most famous of South America's lost explorers, of spotting a 68-foot anaconda, but he explains that the most feared creature of the Amazon is the bushmaster, "commonly twelve feet in length, enormous for a pit viper, and the quantity of its peculiar venom so great that even if a quantity of serum was at hand, a sufficient amount could not be transmitted to the victim in time to save his life" (*CF,* 54). And, like every traveller in the Amazon, Matthiessen must comment upon the notorious piranha, confirming the prevailing notion that the fish "almost never attacks except when there is blood or other wound fluid in the river . . ." (*CF,* 136). He tells of catching a two-pound specimen in the same place in the river where he had been swimming only five minutes before. Yet the following day a child swimming nearby, with an open thumb cut, was rushed from the water, bleeding from a piranha bite in the exact area of the unhealed wound.

The animals are one thing, but Matthiessen is at his nonfictional best describing the forest itself and its spell:

> In New England one walks quite gradually into a wood, but not so in the jungle. One steps through the wall of the tropic forest, as Alice stepped through the looking glass; a few steps, and the wall closes behind. The first impression is of the dark, soft atmosphere, an atmosphere which might be described as "hanging," for in the great tangle of leaves and fronds and boles it is difficult to perceive any one plant as a unit; there are only these hanging shapes draped by lianas in the heavy air, as if they had lost contact with the earth. And this feeling is increased by the character of the earth itself, which is quite unlike the thrifty woodland floor at home; here the tree boles erupt out of heaped-up masses of decay, as if the ground might be almost any distance beneath. The trees themselves are so tumultuous and strange that one sees them as a totality, a cumulative effect, scarcely noticing details. (*CF,* 38)

One could go on quoting from the book's wealth of anecdote, observation, and commentary. In fact, its reportorial interest supports my hypothesis about the wellsprings of its material. At least, that is, up to the midpoint of the book.

At that juncture, something radically different happens to the narrative that rattles my hypothesis. There Matthiessen's aimless trip becomes a journey. In the bar of the Gran Hotel Mercedes in Pucallpa, Matthiessen meets a man who claims to have discovered in the jungle the fossil of a jaw so huge that no existing creature would explain its origin. Matthiessen knows enough by now not to trust stories told in South American bars, but another witness confirms the jaw's existence, and Matthiessen's curiosity and sense of adventure are piqued. When he leaves that little river town at the edge of the wilderness, Matthiessen has a mission; his story thereby assumes direction and accrues a mythic dimension. The giant fossil is the principal object of his quest; but, after that, Matthiessen and his friend, Andres Porras, plan to plunge deeper into the mystery of the forest by seeking a previously unreported Inca ruin, and perhaps, thereafter, by visiting a wild tribe of Amahuaca Indians. All three objectives of his quest, with their connections to ancient history and the primitive, deepen its meaning by adding the dimension of a search for origins.

The entire second half of the book details these quests and the questors' near-fatal adventure. One reviewer even suggested that this should have been the whole book. Indeed the work becomes not only more focused and lively, but it enlarges in meaning as well. The running of the Pongo rapids (so treacherous that Matthiessen believes he and his partner were the first white men to survive their fury during the rainy season) in search of the ancient mandible takes on the classic motif of a passage through danger for a purpose. The jaw becomes the grail, Matthiessen and his companion, pilgrims. Man risks death to search for evidence of early life. This is the trial by water that the hero must undergo in order to prove worthy of his task.

Eventually, they succeed by a combination of courage, skill (that Matthiessen attributes to his Indian guides), and luck. They find the grail and return it to Pucallpa. It is gigantic and a true fossil. One quest is accomplished. The book ends, however, with a failure, as the author is unable to export the huge fossil from Peru to a paleontologist for exact identification and preservation. The trip to the supposed ruins is left unattempted, the wild Amahuacas unapproached, the author deciding that he had pushed his luck far enough. Yet Matthiessen feels he will return to the jungle, for he has a "strong sense that something mysterious exists here" (*CF*, 264). It is a mystery, however, not easily identified or explained, for the whole expedition of the jaw lies behind a quasi-hallucinatory veil, perhaps not totally unrelated to the jungle potion, "*soga de muerte*," or "vine of death," that Matthiessen imbibes before leaving Pucallpa. And then there is the image of the cloud forest—trees engulfed in mountain clouds, experiences hidden behind a cloud of mystery, a cloud of unknowing.

Matthiessen is content to let the whole experience stand for itself— eschewing an attempt to sum up its significance or to generalize his experience, allowing the final image of the bone, the giant *mandibula* "sinking slowly beneath man's detritus on the steaming banks of the Ucayali" (*CF*, 269), to symbolize the result. As in other Matthiessen nonfictional adventures, the true discoveries are unpredictable, the rewards unexpected while in pursuit of something else. Reflecting on the harrowing Pongo trial by water, Matthiessen says, "we may have had a more significant adventure than the ones we originally sought" (*CF*, 212).

The book, with evident disregard for my hypothesis about nonfiction, assumes clearly mythic overtones, dealing with mankind's search for the mystery of the wild, a mystery that will always remain beyond the ken of the civilized mind. And yet, in this search, man has moments of vision, moments of sight into the still river of the past.

This is nonfiction clearly operating beyond the realm of anecdote, travelogue, or fact, and in the realm of meaning. And to take the larger perspective, other Matthiessen books do the same thing, most notably his National Book Award–winning *The Snow Leopard*.[6] Suddenly, further examples of nonfiction's explanatory dimension flood the picture: Thoreau's *Walden,* Solzhenitsyn's *The Gulag Archipelago,* C. S. Lewis's *Surprised by Joy,* Simone de Beauvoir's *The Second Sex,* Augustine's *Confessions.* Yet I think something of the hypothesis can be salvaged, for in all these cases the events have intrinsic significance, especially to the writer, who is a principal participant in the action, or at least in the agony behind the action. Had Matthiessen's trip ended without the bar conversation and the search for the jaw, his book would still have been good reading, informative and involving. His tale, however, would not have signified. Nonfiction, then, can only move into the realm of meaning if the action it reports on has intrinsic meaning. This is clear from the two radically different parts of *The Cloud Forest,* as well as from the above examples (and all others I can think of) of nonfiction that interprets life. These examples also indicate that nonfiction will more readily accrue significance if the author is a major participant in the action, although a nonparticipating author conceivably could weave a significant tale from the meaningful actions of others. Fiction, on the other hand, is not contingent upon the events' significance or the author's participation, for in fiction the imagination can create significance out of the most banal and distant of experiences. Nonfiction has more contingencies, but it too can say: "I will show you fear in a handful of dust," *if* it is really dust being shown (i.e., the beginnings and endings of things) and especially if the writer tells about the time he or she actually held it in hand.

At Play in the Fields of the Lord

Although Matthiessen's *Cloud Forest* has mythic overtones, much is left unprobed. Like Matthiessen, who did not find the Inca ruins and the wild tribe, it stops short of something that the author evidently felt while there. In fact, I believe Matthiessen's very absence of direct experience of the Amahuacas partly led to his remarkable fictive journey into the experience of a wild tribe, the Niarunas, in *At Play in the Field of the Lord* (1965). In a sense, the novel may be the return Matthiessen felt he would make to the Peruvian Amazon when he departed at the end of *The Cloud Forest.* The earlier book provides the factual background, intellectual framework, and emotional impetus that contribute to the full-scale enterprise of the imagination that becomes the novel.

The novel is set among the wild rivers and forests of southeastern Peru, toward the Brazilian border, that was the scene of Matthiessen's most extensive adventure in *The Cloud Forest*. Madre de Dios, the jungle capitol of the novel, and its satellite settlement, Remate de Males, are real places in Peru, but they are not where they are in the novel. Suffice it to say that Matthiessen blends a number of jungle capitols, outposts, and missions for his fictitious locales, and the names themselves, Mother of God and End of Evils, are chosen for their thematic suggestiveness rather than their literal correspondence. The Espiritu River of the novel looks like the Inuya River of the chronicle, and the fictitious Niaruna tribe is partly modeled on the wild Amahuacas that Matthiessen had wanted to visit. But novelists, of course, are bandysnatchers—it goes with the territory—so Matthiessen draws Niaruna customs from a variety of Amazonian tribes, most notably the Machiguengas, Mayorumas, and Carajas, ascribing to the Niarunas the latter's ritual rape of any woman who ventures near a tribal dance of the males.

Likewise, specific anecdotes about the people, habitats, and customs related in *The Cloud Forest* surface in the novel. For example, in the former, Matthiessen tells of a pretty Machiguenga girl who let one of her twin babies starve to death, explaining that "her maternal negligence, cruel and unnatural by our lights, is by no means uncommon among the jungle Indians, who are more practical about such matters, especially when a shortage of food or even a simple disinclination to assume the burden make[s] children undesirable" (*CF,* 221). The incident is reflected in the novel when Lewis Moon's sometime bedpartner, an Indian woman, has twins and buries the girl twin alive, not only without compunction, but even with some surprise at Moon's objection. After all, it is only animals, she defends herself, that have multiple litters, and she would have been disgraced before the tribe were her twins revealed, for she is no animal. The manner in which this anecdote from the chronicle is resituated in the novel is typical. Countless details from the first book make the novel convincingly realistic.

The real question, however, is not the similarity of the two books, but their difference. What part of Matthiessen's experience was not absorbed by the chronicle? Whence the inspiration for a novel? And why this particular story? Why the thick jungles of Peru rather than the harsh coasts of Tierra del Fuego? Why Lewis Meriwether Moon, a half-breed Cheyenne, as principal? Why missionaries reaching after converts instead of timbermen in search of profit?

Milan Kundera, in *The Art of the Novel,* defines the novel as a meditation on existence as seen through the medium of imaginary characters.[7] His definition helps to sort out fictional from nonfictional processes in

Matthiessen's two books, and, by extension, helps to differentiate the fictive from the reportorial impulse. *The Cloud Forest* contains a meditation on existence in its presentation of Matthiessen's experiences in search of the ancient jawbone, but, despite this, the book is only accidentally and partially meditative. That is, the meditation arises from the events and is, therefore, ontologically secondary to them. The book, by its very disparate nature, illustrates this. The whole first section, while it contains observations and reflections that could be the beginning of a meditation on existence, is unable to sustain that meditative quality because it must keep up with the pace of the facts. And even the final section's meditation, based upon the narrator's personal quest, is limited by the literal import of the events narrated. In other words, Matthiessen has no choice but to leave us wondering about the mysteriousness of the wild, for he had gone only so far in his canoe. The thoughts and experiences of *The Cloud Forest* are like seeds, some of which required a further and deeper imaginative planting—in this case, in the fields of the Lord.

In three or four places within *The Cloud Forest,* Matthiessen alludes to the missionary work of the American Protestant Fundamentalists and of Catholic priests among the Indians of South America, mentioning the not-altogether-beneficial effects of this work upon the tribes. Matthiessen gingerly refrains from intruding his own beliefs into any discussion of the harvest of souls, but he does at one point allude to his affinity with the atheistic Albert Camus, and at another he mentions his refusal to lead a prayer at the start of a plane trip with a group of fundamentalist missionaries. On the latter occasion he reflects on the faith of his companions: "How serene these people are—as if religion were a state of shock . . . that good men like these are driven into by the spectacle of reality" (*CF,* 129). Comments like these leave the reader of the chronicle curious about the motivations of these serene missionaries, who in recent years have converted large numbers of South Americans to a fundamentalist Christianity—a curiosity that will be satisfied by the fuller, more imaginative probings of the novel. At another point in *The Cloud Forest,* Matthiessen raises the issue of the actual benefits of this evangelization. One of the missionaries himself "sadly concedes [to the author] that the exposure of a primitive tribe to missionaries, however successful—because of the care, generosity, and devotion of the missionaries, the tribe is almost always benefited at the outset—is followed more often than not by its extinction, through subsequent exploitation, mixed breeding, alcohol, and disease that arrive not with the advent of the Word but with civilization" (*CF,* 132–3).

These two reflections about missionaries, civilization, and Indians, along with Matthiessen's experience of the wild and his unaccomplished desire to visit the wild Amahuacas, are the windows from *The Cloud Forest* that look out upon the larger imaginary land of *At Play in the Fields of the Lord,* an impressive novel. It is a tale woven thick with the sinews of jungle, unfamiliar Indian ways, uncharted land, missionary zeal, burned-out nomadism, corruption, sacrifice, and search. The novel gathers together the chronicle's disparate and unsustained observations about certain tribes, their evangelization by Catholics and Protestants, and threats to their purity from the concomitant civilizing process to weave a meditation on the nature and importance of indigenous wildness itself and on the motivations of civilized men and women who come to these wild places both bringing what they have and searching for something they lack (these prove within the novel to be inextricably bound).

It begins innocently enough as a story about two soldiers of fortune—their names and motto scrawled on the fuselage of their light plane: Wolfie & Moon, Inc. / Small Wars and Demolition—stranded in the boondocks of Peru with wide-eyed, praise-the-Lord missionaries, a patient and wary old Catholic priest, a corrupt, self-serving commandante, and an assorted cast of tame Indians, half-breeds, and wild Indians. The work becomes a search for meaning through its powerful characters, each one etched in unique postures: Leslie Huben, the fundamentalist missionary ("We thank the Lord for this tractor") whose burning mission leads him to risk all and block out reality to reach the Niarunas; Huben shrinks in stature, his wife tells him, because his beliefs preclude true charity. Andy Huben, his wife and the desire of every man in the story, who runs on the fuel of her husband's faith until he diminishes and leaves her to come to terms with her own emptiness. Martin Quarrier, a true seeker, who as a missionary comes to realize the folly of the enterprise through the pain of his son's death, but who never capitulates, a large man who faces danger with courage and who finds a permanence in his principles before he is brutally murdered. Hazel Quarrier, who breaks completely after her son's death, becoming a parodic voice of Christian platitudes and shocking blasphemies. Wolfie, the ultimate soldier of fortune, who has a thief's honor and a thief's love for his sidekick, Moon. And Moon himself, the half-breed Cheyenne who never really had a home after he, his people's hope, left college in disgrace. He lost so much that he has come to the point of not caring, and that makes him truly unafraid. In his vision under the influence of the "vine of death," he leaves the white settlement and flies off to the east where he parachutes to the Niaruna as Kisu-man, the Great God of the Rain.

The whole world of the wild Indian tribe, its culture, religion, superstitions, ways of living, breeding, celebrating, and dying, is opened up to us by having Kisu-Moon gradually inducted into the tribe. Our respect grows for the wild ways of men and women at one with nature when we see the thoroughness of their acclimatization. The book does not romanticize the Indians, for we see them, as does Moon, at times wickedly cruel and pathetically stupid. But they do have something we have lost through our advanced civilization. And while the book doesn't say that savage life is best, it does imply that the savages are better off in their natural state than they will be when and if they are tamed, Christianized, and basically broken, for then they will be of neither one culture nor the other, but rather an ancillary of the white man.

The novel, like *The Cloud Forest,* provides an amazing wealth of detail about the wilderness, but more, it has a vision that asks the major questions about ideals, suffering, love-lust, courage, and true morals. It shows a path of central humanity that crosses wild and tame, but the crossing is dangerous and one can have no assurances of peace and attainment apart from the drifting and finding of the moment. Somehow, Matthiessen suspends questions of the truth of beliefs and concentrates more on the effects of beliefs on people who may not absorb them anyway. Perhaps Padre Xantes is the most universal voice of the book's tolerance in his words to Wolfie, Andy, and the others. His message is that there is a God of love, one God, who looks upon our theological differences with some bemusement as we work so seriously, instead of playing, in the fields of the Lord.

The comments of *The Cloud Forest* are windows to the fields of the Lord; the experience of *The Cloud Forest* is the beginning of a search into the nature and importance of wildness that is *At Play in the Fields of the Lord,* which is able to deepen isolated reflections from the chronicle by fleshing them out with imaginary characters. For example, the novel can take the fictitious Lewis Meriwether Moon much further back to the primitive than Peter Matthiessen had ever gone. As Moon becomes one with the Niaruna and eventually seeks to prevent the tribe's domestication by the missionaries, our sympathy is aroused for the Indians and their customs, not in some Rousseauvian Romantic way, but simply in appreciation for a viable way of life, deserving respect. Having achieved only a small part of his desire to fathom the mystery of the forest and its peoples in *The Cloud Forest,* Matthiessen accomplishes an enormously complex creation of a primitive native tribe, complete with metaphysical outlook, religious tradition, social structure, language, environmental adaptation, customs, ethics, and rituals. So convincing, so believable is his Niaruna tribe that—had not one known otherwise—one would have imagined that Matthiessen did indeed visit and live for a while with the fierce Amahuaca or another hostile tribe. This is truly an extraordinary achievement.

Within the novel, Matthiessen convinces the reader that an overlapping of motive exists between the missionary in his over-reaching idealism and the soldier of fortune in his burned-out cynicism; that there is something in the wild, something in the untamed parts of the world, that calls out to the explorer in all people. And he meditates on this inclination in the novel more thoroughly than the literalness of his own experiences allows him in the chronicle. Martin Quarrier and Lewis Moon come together in their appreciation for and devotion to the Niaruna near the end of the novel, Quarrier planning to exchange his missionary work for ethnological study that will include helping the tribe with medicine and food, Moon intending to organize the wild tribes in order to protect them against the guns of the Commandante and the government. Quarrier even offers to accompany him in this task. Unfortunately, Quarrier is killed, but ironically by the "civilized" and "Christianized" Indian Yoyo, not by the wild Indians to whom he is drawn. Symbolically, the murder weapon is a mission machete that has a cross carved in its haft.

The Impulses of Fact and Meditation

To return again to the focus on the different impulses that result in books of different natures, we have seen that many of the novel's concerns are glimpsed through brief and sporadic passages in the chronicle. However, the latter book is guided by an entirely different impulse, the impulse of fact. Evidently Matthiessen, in the course of reporting his experiences to the *New Yorker* audience and then to the general public in book form, was impelled into further meditation on certain aspects of reality that he had encountered. This reflection demanded a novel because only a novel allowed him the freedom to focus and project the complexity of his thoughts. On the most elementary level, Matthiessen had to make up a story because it didn't actually happen. But paradoxically, he could make up this story only because it was what really happened to him in South America. That is, it was the aspect of the whole experience that affected his depths, where the meanings are.

The enterprise of writing a novel is so monumental that an author of necessity writes largely from life-themes, from personal concerns that carry over into every part of the author's life. The process is inescapable, even for a writer like Nabokov, who ostensibly uses his characters as pawns in a chess game. His novels become reflections of his vision of life as game and novelist as inventor. Thus every novelist takes something from within, a personal vision independent of the particular occasion for his novel. In Matthiessen's case, it is a vision of life as quest and spiritual search, of man as nomad—Lewis Meriwether Moon but also Peter Matthiessen, who himself has traveled the continent of South America, if not as a mercenary-soldier of fortune, at least as a mercenary-writer, employee of William Shawn and the *New Yorker*.

Matthiessen's two books illustrate the essential difference between the fictive and the reportorial instincts. The former is essentially meditative, employing characters and action as a medium of that meditation. The latter can be meditative as well, but—as is exemplified by the two parts of *The Cloud Forest*—it is only accidentally so (in the scholastic sense), for nonfiction is dependent on its sequence of events. If this sequence, as in the first half of the chronicle, has no sustained significance, neither does the narrative. If, as is the case with the book's second part, the facts pull themselves together, the nonfiction is of an altogether different and deeper sort. And what about Matthiessen's, or any author's, motive in writing in one genre rather than the other? I believe it to be a question of the precedence of fact or the precedence of vision. Some experiences are too real, perhaps too harrowing and too entwined with one's identity in time and place, to be submitted to fictive transformation. They demand nonfiction.[8] This is why most mountain literature is nonfiction. Other experiences are too visionary, too meditative, too significant to be submitted to the tyranny of fact. They demand fiction. This explains why even heavily autobiographical stories, like Melville's early sea voyages and Hemingway's pilgrimage to the Pamplona bullfights, become novels. Of course, I am speaking here as if nothing other than the experience itself were a motivating factor, which in the real world of making a living by writing is not always the case. At any rate, we know that Peter Matthiessen had not one but two experiences in South America, and we are the richer for them both.

Chapter Five

Explorer of the Wild Places

Under the Mountain Wall, Oomingmak, Blue Meridian,
The Tree Where Man Was Born, Sand Rivers

The 1960s was a decade of extensive travel for Peter Matthiessen. Four of the above books, all nonfiction, resulted from trips during this time to some of the remotest and most primitive corners of the earth. His journeys to a Stone Age tribe in New Guinea, to an austere island in the Bering Sea, to the icy South Australian seas, to the plains of Serengeti and the Selous Game Reserve in East Africa show Matthiessen at his most adventuresome. Yet, as one reviewer noted, his voyages have not been impelled "by some silly man-against-the-elements ideal. His central thrust has been to celebrate the virtues of lost cultures, to praise the excellence of life apart from human life, to bear witness to creation vanishing."[1] The trips are all chronicled in tones respectful, even reverential, towards the mystery of nature's disappearing domain. Like the speaker in Wallace Stevens's poem "Anecdote of the Jar," Matthiessen sees the touch of civilization altering the wilderness, rendering it "no longer wild," taking "dominion everywhere." The civilizing impulse, Matthiessen has learned from his travels, like the jar in the poem, "did not give of bird or bush."

Matthiessen's obvious respect for the untamed and uncivilized separates him from the old-time bearers of the white-man's burden, colonizers and missionaries, who, even when their motives were purest, looked down patronizingly upon the natives, their customs and habitats. Nevertheless, the best of these colonial and missionary explorers, in carrying either "civilization" or "the good news" to the wild, possessed an altruism absent in Matthiessen.

Instead of approaching the wild with missionary altruism, Matthiessen comes with humility and awe, seeking to learn and be restored rather than to teach and to heal. His adventures are adventures of the inner self. Nature is his teacher, especially its great primitive forces that have shaped the world and its peoples. He is a direct descendant of the 19th-century American Transcendentalists in his belief in the restorative, pedagogical, and spiritual powers of nature. Like Thoreau, who "went to the woods . . . to live deliberately," and Emerson, who said, "To the intelligent, nature converts itself into a vast promise, and will not be rashly explained,"[2] Matthiessen has gone to nature for enlightenment and peace. Looking back upon the many journeys to nature's depths, Matthiessen admits, "I already had what Kierkegaard called 'the sickness of infinitude,' wandering from one path to another with no real recognition that I was embarked upon a search . . ." (*SL*, 43).

During this decade of travel, Matthiessen's search involved other kinds of trips as well, for it was the time of his experimentation with LSD and other drugs. Drugs too were ventures into the wild, offering, as Matthiessen thought at the time, "another way of seeing, and not in the slow labor of ascetic discipline but in cool efficiency and speed, as in flight through air" (*SL*, 44). The new way of seeing, however, would prove to be no more visionary than the trickery of a magic show or the illusion of kaleidoscope. In his essay "The Poet," Emerson had warned about the poet's temptation to substitute the illusory experience of opiates for the true poetic experience. After nearly a decade of experimentation, Matthiessen came essentially to the same position, admitting that "here and there a blissful passage was attained that in my ignorance I took for religious experience" (*SL*, 44). He abandoned the use of drugs in the late 1960s, convinced that the magic-carpet ride they induced, while effective in transporting him back to early childhood trauma, had no connection with reality, that "lacking the temper of ascetic discipline, the drug vision remains a sort of dream that cannot be brought over into daily life" (*SL*, 47). As his experimentation with drugs waned and then ended, Matthiessen's interest in Zen grew. Since this subject is treated in chapter 8, suffice it to say here that Matthiessen's spiritual and physical movements of the 1960s go hand in hand.

His motivations for his expeditions are the same as those of his inner searching. He is driven by a desire to know, to merge with the other in an act of contemplation, the most intense kind of knowing. Like Adam in the Garden of Eden, Matthiessen delights in the otherness of creation around him; and also like Adam, he delights in his human power of language, the ability to name these creatures. The contemplative and linguistic acts constitute his essential stance in relation to nature's wild domains. His journeys are fueled by the desire to be at one with nature and to tell about it. The former demands receptivity and openness, the willingness to wait upon the dispositions of the wild, hoping that one will see the great white shark or the snow leopard or the rhinoceros. The latter requires the exertion of control by means of language over the revelations that have been vouchsafed.

Because Matthiessen is at heart a novelist, despite his greater number of nonfiction books, his linguistic impressions of his journeys into the wild often accrue an imaginative dimension. Out of his encounters with the wilderness there collectively emerges a story with a plot, theme, and characters. Individual renderings of this story vary from trip to trip, with different shades of emphasis and tone, but the essentials are the same.

The plot is of a planet evolving in Darwinian fashion, the stronger and faster and smarter surviving in a gradual and natural manner, until the arrival of man with his superior tools and intelligence. As man himself becomes more advanced, refining his instruments and living over and against nature in more highly artificial environments, he begins to destroy the old patterns and many of the existing creatures, out of all proportion to his needs. Man's technology is irresistible and his callousness lamentable since he is *sapiens* and should know better. He destroys not only for survival, as do the other creatures, but directly for profit and sport as well, and indirectly because he cannot control all of the consequences of his technological advancement, consequences like oil spills from megatankers and pollutants from industrial waste.

The characterization of man in this story, however, is complex, for he exists in varying states of civilization and wildness, although the latter has been gradually disappearing as a result of the very dynamism of civilization itself. In his least civilized states, like the Kurelu tribe of New Guinea, man is least destructive of his natural environment despite his killing for survival. In his partly civilized forms, like some of the Indians of South America or certain tribes of East Africa, he is increasingly destructive, burning the rain forests to plant crops, slaughtering elephants to barter their ivory, and poaching onto the game reserves for meat of any kind. Man, in this in-between stage, is a victim, however, as much as a culprit. One can hardly blame starving Africans for killing "rare" beasts in order to live or destitute Brazilian peasants for trying to create arable land. In fact, the intermediate stage between civilized and wild is the unhappiest lot of all, for it means dissatisfaction with the old and subjugation by the new. The most culpable are those who are most privileged and still do not care, those who continue to demand ivory trinkets despite the dwindling numbers of elephants, those who litter the seas with twenty-mile nets, wantonly killing everything that comes their way. Mankind is the collective villain, but there are definite shades of guilt in Matthiessen's characterization of the human family. And there are even some heroes as well, enlightened preservationists who have gone out of their way to protect the natural environment. Some of the men with whom Matthiessen has traveled fall into this category, men like Brian

Nicholson, who labored for years to improve the Selous Game Reserve in Tanzania, or John Teal, who initiated the project to capture some of the wild musk ox in an effort to preserve and breed them domestically, or George Schaller, the wildlife biologist who was with Matthiessen on the Serengeti Plain and in the Himalayas.

Part of Matthiessen's story, of course, involves danger and suspense; for, in order to observe the wild, one must approach it, and that means risk. The wild, by its nature, is unpredictable; because Matthiessen's impulse is to seek out the very wildest and most primitive parts of the wilderness, an air of danger permeates his story. This element of expedition writing has always been a major part of its appeal, and it accounts for some of Matthiessen's popularity. In order to see things up close, he and his company must expose themselves to the perils of wild peoples, wild places, and wild creatures. He runs treacherous rapids in Peru. He looks directly into the dead-eyed, razor-toothed smile of the great white shark in the South Australian seas. He faces musk ox, rhinoceros, and hippopotamus at point-blank range.

His willingness to undergo risk increases the value of the story's theme, for the object of the quest, the wilderness itself, enlarges in value as more is chanced to know and understand it. The risk itself is never handled with chest-beating braggadocio or tight-lipped code heroism. Matthiessen, in fact, mostly removes his ego from the story, content to observe what others are doing; or if he is directly involved, content to draw attention to the object observed rather than to himself in danger. The emphasis is not on the conflict between man and nature, although that conflict is frequently present because of the often perilous situation itself. Danger, for Matthiessen, is a means to an end, and that end is knowledge or, in its purest state, contemplation. While this contemplative impulse may be hard to separate from his wanting something to write about—for Matthiessen always goes into these adventures knowing he will report on them—they are clearly distinct motivations. One does not feel that Matthiessen puts himself into dangerous situations in order to inject suspense into his books. On the contrary, one feels that he pursues his contemplative interests despite the risks. In fact, he continually underplays the danger in ticklish situations, emphasizing the beauty and awesomeness of the creature observed or the practical necessity of the action taken. Matthiessen is no thrill seeker. Or rather the ultimate thrill for him is not danger itself, but union with the wild mysteries of nature.

At base this is a religious experience. Union with the other is both the object of Zen meditation and a mystical castle of Christian contemplation. In his classic treatise on religious experience, *The Idea of the Holy,* Rudolf Otto identifies this oneness with the mysterious as a fundamentally religious impulse. Otto suggests that mystery, in its natural sense, would simply mean a secret or puzzle, something incomprehensible and unexplained. Yet "taken in the religious sense, that which is 'mysterious' is—to give it perhaps the most striking expression—the 'wholly other' . . ., that which is quite beyond the sphere of the usual, the intelligible, and the familiar, which therefore falls quite outside the limits of the 'canny', and is contrasted with it, filling the mind with blank wonder and astonishment."[3] Matthiessen had a seminally religious experience, in Otto's sense of the "wholly other," when he was on board a navy troop ship in the Pacific in World War II. Alone for over eight hours in a storm, Matthiessen became one with the elements. He later recounted: "I lost my sense of self, the heartbeat I heard was the heart of the world, I breathed with the mighty risings and declines of earth, and this evanescence seemed less frightening than exalting" (*SL,* 43). In a sense this experience foreshadows all the other great contemplative moments in his subsequent journeys to nature's untamed dominions. Like it, the other adventures are self-effacing experiences, involving both danger and total absorption. Each book, of course, tells its own variation of this general story with its own peculiar techniques and versions of the contemplative moment.

Under the Mountain Wall: A Chronicle of Two Seasons in Stone Age New Guinea

In 1961 Matthiessen was a part of the Harvard-Peabody Expedition to a remote corner of western New Guinea, the Baliem Valley that sits under the peaks of the Snow Mountains. The purpose of the expedition was to live among a tribe of aborigines, the Kurelu, as yet uncontacted by civilized man, and to "film and record their wars, rituals, and daily life with a minimum of interference, in order that a true picture of a Stone Age culture—one of the few in which both war and agriculture are important—might be preserved."[4] A film, *Dead Birds,* was made from the expedition by its leader, Robert Gardner. And in telling his account, Matthiessen purposely imitates the camera's eye as well; for his intention is "to describe a lost culture in the terrible beauty of its pure estate" (*UMW,* xiv). As a result, no mention is made of the expedition members, and no description of the tribe's first reactions to the white man other than Matthiessen's comment in the Preface that it was "affecting and sad and funny" (*UMW,* xiv). Matthiessen's narrative is unblinkingly upon the tribe members themselves, their interactions and customs, and he tells it without intervention or commentary. They are the object of his inquiry; and in studying their life-style, he peers back into the past with his contemplative admiration.

The method must have required enormous discipline, and it was well-conceived. What emerges is the fulfillment of Matthiessen's intention: a portrait of a people totally uninfluenced by civilization. He takes us to war with the Kurelu and to their funerals, marriages, births, quarrels, farming, building, and daily routines. Theirs is a life built around war, power, and clan. And, while certain of the commonplaces of their life seem cruel and unnatural by our lights, such as the ritualized cutting off of fingers in mourning or the killing of "enemy" children and women in raids, the Kurelu appear totally content with life. They and their environment are one. War itself is a commonplace, and the identity of the Kurelu is actually shaped by it and by their traditional enemy, the Wittaia. War is partly a phenomenon of revenge and partly a ritual of sport and manhood. While its occasion is always the most recent wrongs inflicted by the enemy, it has rules and ceremony. Before actual battle, the two sides "would dance out and feign attacks, whirling and prancing to display their splendor. They were jeered and admired by both sides and were not shot at, for display and pan-oply were part of war, which was less war than ceremonial sport, a wild, fierce festival" (*UMW,* 10–11).

Of all Matthiessen's books, *Under the Mountain Wall* is the most documentary in method. Individuals, of course, do emerge. U-mue, by the amount of attention he gets, seems to have been a bit of a scoundrel and a favorite of the author, and Wereklowe proves admirable in his courage and cunning. But the details that stick in one's mind are the customs them-selves, the marriage and funeral ceremonies, the pig celebration, the wearing of the horim (an elongated gourd worn as an erect extension of the penis), the frowning on abortion for the married but the acceptance of it in the un-married, the commonness of wife-rape and pig-theft, and, overwhelmingly, the details of the wars and skirmishes themselves. The book has pictures, many of them by Matthiessen himself, and part of the interest is in seeing what the individuals actually look like. The index makes the work quite ac-cessible for what I imagine to be its principal use: as a reference work for students of anthropology.

As I said, Matthiessen lets the story of the Kurelu practically tell itself. The author's final comment of his Preface, however, unambiguously shows how he feels about the eventual invasion of the aborigines' space that is begun by the expedition's contact. He says, "The armed patrols and mis-sionaries invaded their land on the heels of the expedition, and by the time this account of them is published, the proud and warlike Kurelu will be no more than another backward people, crouched in the long shadow of the white man" (*UMW*, xiv). Undoubtedly, Matthiessen is right in his assessment; and, from his observations of the Kurelu, a picture has indeed been painted of "terrible beauty." The tribe, for all its backwardness, is complete, an entity unto itself and its environment, as content and happy as are the animals themselves.

Two questions do arise, however, in reference to the expedition's effect upon the Kurelu. The first has to do with where the responsibility lies for this initiation of the Kurelu into civilization. Is not the first contact the most telling? And does the motivation of scientific research justify this ingression upon their way of life any more than political or religious motives? The second question deals with Matthiessen's objective narration, as if the events were simply recorded by the camera's eye. How could such a foreign and obtrusive presence as that of a scientific expedition of white men with cameras and other equipment not have changed the picture being observed? As with the Heisenberg principle in physics, it would seem impossible to enter into this field of being without altering it. I can understand Matthiessen's motive for suppressing the story of the interaction between Stone Age people and modern people (he says it has been frequently told in other cases); but then how do we trust his account of the feelings and inner life of the tribespeople without knowing about the rapport or lack of it between them and the author? Could his information have been distorted by coming from only one or two confidants, who themselves had grudges, flights of fantasy, or even maliciousness as motives? All this is only a small caveat, however, about a fine documentary that has the unmistakable feel of honesty and carefulness. Whatever the book's inevitable errors and distortions as a result of method, they could only be minor and incidental to its overall accomplishment.

Oomingmak: The Expedition to the Musk Ox Island in the Bering Sea

Nunivak Island is a small piece of barren land in the Bering Sea that, in 1964, was the only place in Alaska where there was any musk-ox, one of the rarest of the large Ice Age animals left on the earth. That year, Matthiessen joined an expedition to Nunivak led by ecologist and archeologist John Teal and sponsored jointly by the University of Alaska and the Institute of Northern Agricultural Research with the intention of capturing a number of musk-ox calves "to form the nucleus of a permanent domestic herd."[5]

Teal was convinced that the musk-ox could do much for the Inuit economy as a food source and as a supplier of a wool (*qiviut*) that is superior to cashmere.

The book resulting from the expedition, *Oomingmak* (1967), is very brief, only 85 pages, and the text moves with a clear purpose: to narrate the capture of the musk-ox calves, beginning with the flight to Nunivak and the preparations for the hunt. At first, it is hard going. The place is bleak. The musk-ox, in their circular defense formation, are more than a match for the scare-and-scatter techniques of the crew. The basic plan is to corner a small family of musk-ox near the sea, to scare the adults into deep water, and tackle a calf or two. The method is touch and go. They capture a few, but more often than not the musk-ox break through their ranks, or the bulls and cows simply refuse to leave the calves, backing their potential captors away. Since time is important, a decision is made to expedite matters by bringing in a helicopter. This proves successful, and the requisite number of musk-ox are easily isolated and captured, although with considerably less elation among the men than after their previous scattered success.

When Matthiessen says, "The musk-ox were beaten," one detects the remark is said with tongue in cheek. The irony is, however, pointed at himself as well as his fellow expedition members. One tends to think of Matthiessen as a bleeding-heart do-gooder because of his attitudes about nature, but the objectivity of his reporting consistently eschews sentimentalism. In fact, as a bearer of civilization and a part of projects that, while their ultimate intentions are well-meaning, are themselves ambiguous disturbances of a wild environment, Matthiessen presents the situation fairly and unemotionally. Once, as he reported in *The Cloud Forest*, after he had deplored the common practice of shooting at the abundant caimans (South American crocodiles) in the Espiritu River, Matthiessen eventually gave in and joined the shooting. And in *Oomingmak*, of course, he is part of the crew that disrupts the herds of musk-ox for a domestic breeding scheme.

The heart of this book, however, is its description of and appreciation for the natural environment, especially the musk-ox itself. Although the animal looks more like a bison, it is of the goat-antelope family that includes the European chamois. It was once cosmopolitan throughout the Arctic, ranging in the glacial period as far south as France, where its likeness is etched in cave paintings. It disappeared from Eurasia by the end of the Stone Age, and it is now "confined to remnant populations in northeast Greenland and Arctic Canada, with transplanted herds in Norway, Spitzbergen, and Nunivak" (*O*, 29). The animals are large, very fast, and have an acute sense of sight, making any plan of merciful capture a difficult undertaking.

When they are at a distance they look totally black and impressive, and when they run, "backs rising and falling on the grass horizon, long hair blowing, they seemed to flow across the wind, moving with a grace and speed astonishing in such a heavy animal" (O, 33).

The book is as spare and austere as the island and its people. As with *Under the Mountain Wall*, it does not explore the personalities of the expedition. Matthiessen is satisfied to carve a small cameo out of the events themselves, the expedition's encounter with the Inuit, the musk-ox, and the island itself. The Inuit at Nunivak constitute "the North American Eskimo settlement where the aboriginal culture is most intact" (O, 15). They live pretty much as they have always lived, "trapping and fishing and hunting the whale and seal that pass on their migrations and the walrus and polar bear that drift down out of the Bering Straits on the floes of spring" (O, 16). They are cheerful and friendly, self-sufficient and patient, "generous, merry," and among "the most likeable men on earth" (O, 18). The interactions between the expedition and the natives are smooth and cooperative throughout, although Matthiessen's ear for prejudice notices the helicopter pilot's remarks about "all Eskimos looking alike" and his innate suspicion of the Eskimos' wanting to steal parts off his machine.

The black-and-white photographs in the book, many by Matthiessen himself, help to convey the feeling of the island and its inhabitants. The text could as easily have stood by itself, however, as it did in its original version in the *New Yorker*, as a naturalist tone poem, extolling the unexpected grace and beauty of a place and its creatures isolated by location and weather from the paths of travel.

Blue Meridian

Just two years after his voyage on the *Lydia E. Wilson* out of the Cayman Islands in pursuit of the giant green turtle off the Nicaraguan coast, Matthiessen was again at sea. This time the quest was for the most dangerous creature in the deep, the great white shark. And this time the hunt was not for capturing but for filming the shark in its natural habitat. When well-known diver Peter Gimbel, the organizer of the expedition and director of the movie that would be made of it, *Blue Water, White Death*, invited Matthiessen to join, he jumped at the chance. "This was just something I wanted to do," Matthiessen told me, "It seemed like fun." Fun or not, the extent of Matthiessen's daring was tested by the expedition, for he embarked upon it as a novice diver. After getting his first lesson in Florida, he met Gimbel in Nassau, where he received more advanced preparation in the

Blue Hole, a 180-foot dark well that interrupts the Bahamas' sandy bottom. He was then pronounced ready for the real thing.

Blue Meridian (1971) traces the expedition's search for the great white from preparation in Nassau and inception off the coast of Durban, South Africa, through explorations in the Indian Ocean off Ceylon, to a denouement in the cold waters off Australia's southern coast. Matthiessen had to leave the expedition for about two and a half months, but he fills in the blanks of his absence by means of letters from Gimbel, correspondence from others on board the *Terrier,* and especially the diary of diver Valerie Taylor.

Since many of us share the same natural fascination with this most feared of underwater creatures that induced Gimbel to plan the expedition, this is one of Matthiessen's easiest books to read. Even though no great white shark is found until the final stages of the journey, we are carried along by the anticipation of this always hoped for, always dreaded confrontation. Of course, other sharks, especially the large blues and white tips, as big as fourteen or fifteen feet and man-eaters all, provide their own intrinsic interest, so the filming of their plentiful and frenzied feeding off a whale carcass is exciting. Leaving their protective cages in the midst of hundreds of sharks slashing and ripping off whale meat, "the divers swam in a maelstrom of big sharks, and not once was anyone attacked or even seriously threatened; there is always a first time and they knew it, but it never came."[6] This particular bit of narration culminates in Gimbel actually filming within three or four feet of the sharks clamping on mouthfuls of flesh and tearing them away in great powerful arcs of their bodies.

Matthiessen manages to embellish the straight narrative line of success and failure in locating and filming big sharks with a considerable amount of background about the crew, their interactions on the trip, and lore about sharks, particularly the great white. The principal divers and cameramen emerge as hardworking professionals, driven by a love of the sea and an ambition to excel in their work. Their petty arguments and personality clashes only make the whole enterprise more realistic and more human. Matthiessen was lucky to be allowed the extensive use of Valerie Taylor's candid and lively diary, as well as the dramatic underwater photographs of Peter Lake.

Four and a half months after its beginning, the expedition is put on hold to assess the quality of the film garnered thus far and to convince New York backers to finance a final search near Australia for the still unseen great white. Fortunately, both film executives and sharks cooperate. The crew flies to South Australia in January and sails out of Port Lincoln for one last

go at the great white, which finally appears in the frigid waters of Dangerous Reef. Matthiessen narrates: "we stared into its white oncoming mouth.
'My *God!*' Gimbel shouted, astounded by the sight of his first white shark.
The conical snout and the terrible shearing teeth and the dark eye like a hole
were all in sight, raised clear out of the water. Under the stern, with an
audible *whush,* the shark took a last snap at the bait, then wheeled away;
sounding, it sent the skiff spinning with a terrific whack of its great tail, an
ominous boom that could have been heard a half mile away" (*BM,*
188–89).

In subsequent days, the crew descend and film this and another great
white, staying now in the cages that gave, at least, the veneer of safety.
Matthiessen himself is diving once when a great white slides alongside to
take a piece of bait hung from the nearby ship. He says, "The whole expanse
of its ghostly belly, racked by spasms of huge gulping, was perpendicular
against the bars. I scratched the belly with a kind of morbid sympathy, but
at that instant we were jarred by a thrash of the tail" (*BM,* 199). Had the
party not found and filmed the great white shark, both film and book
would have limped by. As it turns out, however, the vertical movement of
the story reaches its target and the book its climax in the eventual discovery
of this hugely dangerous and mysterious creature of the deep.

The Tree Where Man Was Born

Before he joined the white shark expedition in March 1969, Matthiessen
spent two months in the Serengeti Plains of East Africa. Based upon the
travels and experiences of these two months, as well as on a previous brief
visit to the area in 1961 and a return visit in July 1970, Matthiessen wrote
The Tree Where Man Was Born (1972). The book offers an impression of
the region, its peoples and wildlife, informed by a knowledge of prehistoric
times and by a wide reading in the literature about Africa. Replete with
maps, index, glossary, bibliography, and footnotes, the book is more elaborate than any of the others discussed in this chapter. In fact, it is one of
Matthiessen's most complex and successful nonfictional achievements,
ranking alongside *The Cloud Forest* and *The Snow Leopard* in breadth and
understanding.

The book is organized geographically rather than chronologically, although it draws more on Matthiessen's 1961 visit in the first section and
more on his 1969 and 1970 visits later. As in his other travel books,
Matthiessen is guided by his firsthand impressions of the people, their environment, their history, and the animal life around them. Here, however,

there is a pervasive anthropological focus—a comparing of the ages of peoples, animals, fauna—an interest in beginnings. The framing metaphor of the book is the great baobab tree, said to live to be 2500 years old, the oldest living thing on earth. As he moves around Africa, Matthiessen senses the contrast of old and new, noting: "In every distance stand strange shrouded landscapes of the past and future. The present is wild blowing light, the sun, a bird, a baobab in heraldic isolation, like the tree where man was born."[7] The baobab becomes a symbol of Africa, old, beautiful, dying: "Perhaps the greatest baobab were already full grown when man made red rock paintings at Darashagan. Today young baobab are killed by fires, set by the strangers who clear the country for their herds and gardens, and the tree where man was born is dying out in Hadza Land" (*TWMB*, 396).

The theme is familiar from other Matthiessen explorations in the wild. The old ways and the old peoples are dying out, peoples like the Hadza tribe, believed to be a relic of the Stone Age, barely surviving the encroachments of civilization and the natural peril of a declining wildlife population. The Hadza have no awareness of the wilderness as wilderness because they are a part of it, living for and in the moment and guided by patterns instilled by repetition over the long years. The baobab, according to Hadza myth, figures prominently in the origin of man, for man appeared on the earth by climbing down a baobab tree (*TWMB*, 333).

Like the wild tribes he encountered in South America and New Guinea, the Hadza are better off left alone in their primitive contentment and customs "until a choice that they can make naturally is provided, for this people is acknowledged by all who have met them to be healthy and happy, with no history of epidemic or famine, and able to satisfy all needs in a few hours of each day" (*TWMB*, 337). The government, however, has little tolerance for such an uncivilized people who cannot be administered or taxed, and the sooner their culture vanishes, the sooner progress will be declared. This meeting ground between civilization and the wild is a painful one. The remotest tribes are resented by the authorities for their autonomy and backwardness. The fringes of those tribes who cross over to civilization are looked down upon by other Africans, however, and indeed they are the most forlorn of peoples, dark imitators of less dark imitators of pale ways.

As for the question of conservation of nature and animals, one of Matthiessen's most compelling advocacies, many Africans often could not care less. And, to Matthiessen's credit, he presents their position fairly. Why should people who are hungry care about preserving animals who are potential food sources and who are dangerous as well? Matthiessen observes that the Tanzanian government "endorses the principle of conservation, since conservation seems important to those western countries which are helping it in other ways. But most educated Africans care little about wild animals, which are vectors of the tsetse fly, a threat to crops and human life, and a competitor of livestock, and are also identified emotionally with the white man, white hunters, white tourists, and a primitive past which the new Africans wish to forget" (*TWMB*, 336–67). The Tanzanian President, Matthiessen notes, has complained in reference to the Maasai that "the government cannot afford to keep part of its people as a human zoo for tourists" (*TWMB*, 337).

Matthiessen offers no solution to the depressingly complex problem of the effects of western civilization upon the wilderness and its peoples. If anything, his book serves as a tribute and commentary on the power and beauty of the primitive and a lament that such qualities will indeed be lost to change. He visits the Dinka, Maasai, and Hadza tribes, and he appreciates their variety of life-styles. He visits the wild places of Africa's deserts and forests and mountains and appreciates their beauty and their stunning tranquility. He observes the animals—zebra, lions, buffalo, elephant, rhino, hyena, hyrax—and appreciates their precious, and sometimes threatened, existence.

This is, indeed, one of Matthiessen's most contemplative books. Within it are many moments of stark peace and satisfaction. One such is stronger and more revelatory than the rest. It becomes the central epiphany of the chronicle, answering the as yet unspoken needs of the author in his search through the African wilderness. It occurs while he is with the Hadza, after eating some broiled hyrax and guinea fowl, smoking some of their grewia leaves. Together Matthiessen and the Hadza had been examining ancient cave drawings and talking about them. The Africans at first seem at a loss to explain the drawings, claiming that they come from the Old People or God (Mungu), looking to the faces of Matthiessen and his party to see which explanation they would like to hear. Matthiessen observes: "Our need to *understand* makes them uncomfortable. For people who must live from day to day, past and future have small relevance, and their grasp of it is fleeting; they live in the moment, a very precious gift that we have lost" (*TWMB*, 391). Then Matthiessen himself suddenly relinquishes his quest for explanation and passes over into the moment:

Lying back against these ancient rocks of Africa, I am content. The great stillness in these landscapes that once made me restless seeps into me day by day, and with it the unreasonable feeling that I have found what I was searching for without ever having discovered what it was. In the ash of the old hearth, ant lions have countersunk their traps and wait in the loose dust for their prey; far overhead a falcon—and today I do not really care whether it is a peregrine or lanner—sails out over the rim of rock and on across the valley. The day is beautiful, my belly full, and returning to the cave this afternoon will be returning home. For the first time, I am in Africa among Africans. We understand almost nothing of one another, yet we are sharing the same water flask, our fingers touching in the common bowl. At Halanogamai there is a spring, and at Darashagan are red rock paintings—that is all. (*TWMB*, 391–92)

In this revelatory passage, Matthiessen finds the peace that passes all understanding and all explanation. His search is answered not by the vast knowledge he has accumulated but by the simple experience of oneness with his hosts and their surroundings, which include the records of prehistoric man. For once, Matthiessen does not even care to name the kind of falcon he has observed, the contemplative moment overwhelming the linguistic impulse. Matthiessen once again has discovered that the journey itself brings rewards as unpredictable and satisfying as the sought after encounter with the primitive. This epiphanic moment suggests that while the wilderness may be threatened, something of its nature will never die. We will continue to have it with us if we take the time to notice, for the wilderness is a part of us.

Sand Rivers

Matthiessen went back to East Africa in August of 1979 for another safari, this one further south in Tanzania to the Selous Game Reserve, "said to be the greatest stronghold of large wild animals left on earth."[8] The Selous is the least accessible, least known, and largest game reserve in East Africa, more than four times larger than Serengeti. Matthiessen was accompanied by Maria Eckhart, who was born in Tanzania and who would become Matthiessen's wife in 1981, Tom Arnold, Brian Nicholson, his wife Melva, daughter Sandra, and son Philip, Hugo van Lawick, Richard Bonham, Karen Ross, and Robin Pope. *Sand Rivers* (1981) is about this safari, starting with the whole group together and concluding with Matthiessen and Nicholson's walking safari through roadless areas virtually untrod. It is told in narrative fashion, strictly chronologically, although not in journal form; the text is interspersed with groups of van Lawick's photographs of the African wildlife, echoing the focus of the writing, making the animals more tangible, and resulting in a lavish, physically beautiful work. Some of the pictures of the large animals are striking, such as the one of two hippopotamuses fighting with open jaws. Most of the best shots, however, are of smaller creatures, such as birds or lizards, undoubtedly because van Lawick did not accompany Nicholson and Matthiessen into the deepest part of the Reserve, where the animals were less shy about showing themselves because of their scant contact with man. One unfortunate result is the lack of a single picture of a rhinoceros, the animal that elicits Matthiessen's most admiring contemplation.

Sand Rivers is rich in anecdote and lore, Matthiessen ever the perfect companion on these trips into the wild. He informs us, for example, about the strange geographical range of the giraffe of eastern Tanzania which appears north of the Rufiji River, but not south of it for more than six hundred miles until it reappears beyond the Zambezi River; tells us about a lion that in 1951 killed an estimated one hundred people before it was itself killed by the spear of its last victim; observes all of the wildlife encountered along the journey, especially the birds: "I watch striped kingfishers and a whitebreasted cuckoo-shrike, and listen to a bird high in the canopy that I have never heard before and cannot see; its single note is a loud and clear sad *paow!* Circling it, waiting, listening, I am rewarded at last with the sight of a lifetime species, the pied barbet" (*SR*, 186). The book is peripatetic in form, following the author's footsteps and the observations they occasion.

When these footsteps lead to the deepest parts of the great wilderness, the journey takes the form of a visitation back to the past. For Nicholson, the past means not only primitive Africa, the way it used to be, but as well the time he spent as warden of the Selous Reserve until his resignation in 1973 in frustration with government mismanagement. Since Nicholson had overseen the protective work of establishing the roads and paths that would preserve the Selous in its pristine animal richness, his lament over the changing times becomes a motif of the book. The Tanzanian government has castrated the Game Department, and incompetent local administrators have been more intent on careerist opportunism than on the continuance of maintenance and surveillance. As a result, Nicholson sees his work in shambles, the roads, airports, and paths badly neglected and often unusable, game patrols more interested in sharing spirits with local poachers than in bringing them to justice. Ultimately, he senses the dwindling of the herds of elephant, rhinoceros, buffalo, and other big game. Nicholson's observations have weight because of his experience and his level-headed professionalism. The felt experience of the book doesn't always coincide with his pessimism, however, for Matthiessen reports seeing such a richness of wildlife and is so ecstatic about the unspoiled quality of the area that the reader senses that the animals themselves, apart from governmental incompetence and bureaucracy, are doing fine.

In fact, we see so many animals through Matthiessen's eyes, that somewhere along the line we are ready to say, enough! It is one thing to report on seeing elephants, buffalo, wild dogs, kudu, impala, and so on, and to describe their beauty or danger, but it serves little purpose to repeat these sightings over and over. The following account is typical: "Just after five, we make camp beneath a big tamarind at the river's edge, opposite a grove of high borassus. Upstream, a solitary bull elephant wanders the bank; further on an eland emerges from the trees, very pale against the dark greens of the river forest, and a cow elephant and calf stand at rest in the late afternoon sun, as if lost in some long twilight meditation" (*SR,* 142). Such an account of what animals are sighted and how, when repeated in kind, becomes dull. In fact, when the two men come upon a large rhino and calf only about 10–20 yards away, it should be a climactic moment in the story, especially since afterwards Matthiessen tells his companion, "That was worth the whole safari" (*SR,* 192). But the value of this scene is not proportionately conveyed. It is as if Matthiessen feels he need only name the creatures to convey their importance. Matthiessen loves the animals, the wild, and his entrance into this world, but he also loves to name these creatures, to exert over the Goliath heron and the giant kingfisher the quintessentially human power of language. He is indeed Adam in the Garden, giving the right name to all of the beasts. No doubt, fellow naturalists delight in vicariously naming with Matthiessen, especially the birders, for Matthiessen is at his keenest with the creatures of wing. Unfortunately, one must already be a participant in this hobby in order to delight in the process. If you are not already a bird or animal watcher, too often the sightings sound like a litany or like the in-conversation of music buffs or baseball fans.

Brian Nicholson becomes one of the book's genuine interests. His portrait is both critical and admiring, which is why it is so convincing. Matthiessen himself seems fascinated with the man who comes on so gruffly and intolerantly, even prejudiced against the black Africans, but who by the end of the book has developed into a deeper figure, discussing African politics, life in the wild, friendship, and the Africans he has worked with and admires.

Ultimately *Sand Rivers* is a limited accomplishment. It is certainly competent, informative, and lush. What it mainly lacks, however, is that compelling central image that dominated the other books: the wall that separated the Kurelu and civilization; the shaggy musk-ox itself; the great white shark; and the tree where man was born. The rivers of sand, while they are suggestive of the changing patterns of African life, never become the central focus of a book that meanders itself from place to place and animal to animal.

Chapter Six

Voice of Those Who Cannot Speak for Themselves

Sal Si Puedes, In the Spirit of Crazy Horse, Indian Country, Men's Lives

Matthiessen's defense of endangered wildlife and his admiration for the eroding integrity of primitive peoples were prominent in his previous work. In this next group of books, however, three of them published within three years in the early 1980s, his advocacy of threatened ways of life becomes all the more unequivocal and impassioned. Cesar Chavez, Leonard Peltier, the Indian nations, the fishermen of the South Fork are the heroes of four books that are the most partisan of Peter Matthiessen's career. The subjects are all strong men of action (*Indian Country* involves both sexes, but the men are predominant), wounded by society, leading isolated threatened existences and lacking the one thing Matthiessen has in abundance, the gift of language. During my first visit to Matthiessen's home in Sagaponack in January 1989, he discussed his motivation for these books with reference to Albert Camus's Nobel Prize acceptance speech. Camus upheld the writer's responsibility to speak for those who have no voice to speak for themselves. Matthiessen frankly embraces that responsibility. Chicano farm workers, American Indians, and Long Island haul seiners have all lacked an articulate defense for their beleaguered existences, and Matthiessen assumes the mantle of advocacy in writing about their predicaments. While his previous nonfiction did not avoid taking a stand on issues, never had he been guided as single-mindedly by the espousement of a cause as in these books.

Moral earnestness, then, influences the four books' subject matter and tone, an outgrowth of the conscientiousness that spurred the young Matthiessen to question his silver-spoon upbringing. When he was ten years old, Matthiessen recalls, he sold a precious stamp collection that included the entire Coronation Issue (King George VI) of the British Commonwealth, which had been given to him as a Christmas present by his paternal grandmother. He sold it for a mere pittance, marking "the beginnings of a lifelong uneasiness about unearned privilege that was to become an important factor in my life" ("NY," 60). In both his fiction and nonfiction, Matthiessen has consistently sympathized with the nonintellectual, nonprivileged loner. Cady Shipman, Jacobi, Raditzer, Lewis Moon, and Captain Raib are isolated from society by circumstance and action. And in his expedition literature, Matthiessen consistently has expressed genuine affection for the natives. The sherpa Tukten in *The Snow Leopard* evokes the author's admiration and warmth, emerging as a figure of fascination and emulation. It is no surprise, then, that the subjects of these advocacy books are not intellectuals. Chavez comes across as an instinctive genius of political strategy, but even here, Matthiessen points out the leader's own conviction that his firsthand education from meetings and people was better than formal schooling.

The irony of an intellectual's preoccupation with nonintellectuals should go neither unnoticed nor unexplored in our reading of Matthiessen. Part of the explanation may lie in the author's inherent esteem for silence, immediate experience, and commonness as prime values in life, an estimation distinctly within the American literary tradition of Emerson ("The great gifts are not got by analysis. Everything good is on the highway"[1]), Thoreau ("It is life near the bone where it is sweetest"[2]), and Whitman ("What is commonest, cheapest, nearest, easiest, is Me"[3]). Matthiessen really does believe that "every man is a god in ruin," an Adam bereft of paradise. Why else would he so often seek out in his travels those people least affected by civilization and most in harmony with nature? Matthiessen's personal odyssey toward Zen can also be seen in this light.

Another part of the equation of his esteem for nonintellectuals is his admiration for bravery, daring, and boldness, something that Matthiessen shares with a number of his fellow writers of the 1950s. Perhaps it has to do with being young in a country at war. Hemingway, of course, who came of age in the previous war, glorified courage and established the archetype of the writer as hero. The next generation of James Jones, Irwin Shaw, and Norman Mailer—Matthiessen's seniors who also served in World War II—perpetuated, consciously or not, a literary machismo that held bravery in great value. *Esquire,* "the magazine for men," in which all of these writers published, passed it along. It was in *Esquire* in 1965 that Gay Talese had an article, "Looking for Hemingway," in which he claimed that the *Paris Review* crowd were "obsessed, so many of them, by the wish to know how the other half lives. And so they befriend the more interesting of the odd, avoid the downtown dullards on Wall Street, and dip into the world of the junkie, the pederast, the prizefighter, and the adventurer in pursuit of kicks and literature, being influenced perhaps by that glorious generation of ambulance

drivers that preceded them to Paris at the age of twenty-six" (Talese, 47).
While it would be a mistake to see Matthiessen as cut from a Hemingway
mold (indeed, he professes that he's "always had a great antipathy to
Hemingway's macho ideas"), the emphasis on physical valor is an undeniable connection. In his own youth Matthiessen confesses to a "fascination
with the underside of life" that has led him to such risks as crossing Central
Park at night, "the chance of muggers . . . [giving] spring and vigor to my
step" ("NY," 74). In his expeditions, of course, Matthiessen has repeatedly
exposed himself to dangers, and sheer physical courage is a value at issue in
all five of his novels.

When Matthiessen's concern with courage and his belief in the common
man are joined with his lively social conscience and conviction of the writer's
responsibility to speak for those unable to speak for themselves, it is possible to understand the continuity of this group of books, so different in kind
and subject matter, with Matthiessen's previous work. In all four of these
books, the author uses his gift of language to celebrate and defend the values of cultures at odds with the dynamo of contemporary society and to give
voice and stature to the individuals who seem most closely in touch with
these values.

Sal Si Puedes: Cesar Chavez and the New American Revolution

Cesar Chavez qualifies as a man of primal intensity and depth, an integral man whose crusade on behalf of the farm workers originated in his own
poverty and who is continually recharged by living the simple, poor life of
those he represents. Sal Si Puedes (Escape If You Can) is the name of the
barrio in San Jose where Chavez was living when he began his efforts to un-
ionize the farm workers. By using it in his title (1969), Matthiessen emphasizes the humble origins of the movement begun by one charismatic
individual as a response to the working conditions of a particular industry in
which he had labored. By the end of the book, Matthiessen has recast the
particulars of Chavez's efforts to organize the farm workers and bring the
California grape growers to the bargaining table into the larger terms of "the
new American revolution," an amorphous and optimistic grouping of environmental, labor, and peace efforts that was so much a part of the spirit of
the 1960s. Vietnam peace demonstrations, Saul Alinsky's community organizing, the grape boycott, antipesticide outcry, and Black Panthers crop up
as the social context of what were heady times. Now, some twenty years
later, the term "new American revolution" looks inflated, and the events of

the 1960s, including Chavez's struggle and his widely supported grape boycott, evoke nostalgia and uneasy questions that seem almost more important than the events of the book itself. In retrospect, the revolution was not a
revolution, although the farm workers eventually got their contracts with
the growers, and the country got out of Vietnam. The victories were palpable, but there was no great wave of continuity into a more socially conscious
1970s.

As a part of the history of the sixties and its social upheaval,
Matthiessen's book is a valuable document. It tells from the inside the story
of Chavez's struggles in 1968 and 1969 to organize the farm workers of
California. Matthiessen visited Chavez and observed firsthand his daily
work, his meetings, his telephone calls, his speeches, his family, his friends
and supporters, and the key players in his organization. From the start,
Matthiessen is clear about his sympathy with Chavez and his cause. Yet he
desires to understand both sides and seeks out interviews with the growers,
in some cases modifying his outrage as a result of the response. Nevertheless, he seldom lets his inquiry delve into the problems the growers themselves might have or why they would resist Chavez's unionizing with such
vehemence. As for the workers, the facts themselves cry out for a remedy to
their plight: abysmal working conditions, low wages, lack of benefits, and
safety hazards on the job. The book and its shorter form in the *New Yorker*
must have been helpful in galvanizing support of the grape boycott, which
was eventually successful enough to force the growers to the bargaining
table. The book's reportorial quality, however, with its exhausting detail of
name, event, and conversation makes for dry, dull reading today, in the rear-
view mirror of twenty years. The day-by-day accounts of Chavez's and his
organizers' strategies, the incidents on the picket lines, and the rhetoric of
union meetings are cold news, like yesterday's newspaper.

What is interesting about the book is the portrait of Chavez himself, his
place in the history of the labor movement in the United States and his personal charisma, which ignited an unprecedented nationwide boycott of
grapes. At one point in the account, Matthiessen says that he knew that he
would be impressed by Chavez, even that he would be "organized" by him,
but he did not count on being "startled" by the man's personal power.
Chavez emerges as a kind of saint, a man deeply committed to helping others, not an abstract crusader, but one who sees clearly the extent of his influence and gives himself fully to it. Unlike the officials of other unions,
Chavez and his assistants of the United Farm Workers Organizing Commit-
tee receive no pay. He is a tireless worker, putting in twelve hours a day even
from his bed when his nagging back pain becomes so devastating it forces

him off his feet. And he is a man of the people, making himself available to anyone who wants to see him, constantly organizing whomever he meets. When his union organizers become discouraged, he is buoyant, encouraging them and assuring them of ultimate success. When they are foolish or irresponsible, he is the taskmaster, scolding and admonishing.

Chavez's unreserved commitment to his cause, of course, affects his personal and family life. Matthiessen tells us that he lives a deliberately poor and simple life, not only because he has little and has refused to seek the path of accumulation, but also because he realizes that his lifestyle affects his capability of leadership among the people he seeks to serve. Such a lifestyle would not be possible if Chavez's wife, Helen, were not as committed as he. Naturally she and the children suffer from the limited attention Chavez is able to give to them; but, in Matthiessen's description, the deprivation seems compensated for by the quality of his time with his family. At any rate, it is a choice that Chavez has made, like many of the strategic choices in the course of his organizing, brooking no second guessing. One senses that he is a man so used to a less than perfect world that deprivation, once placed within a larger purpose, could never shake his course of action.

The principal example of this in the book is Chavez's twenty-five-day fast, which brought public attention to his cause and helped mobilize the then struggling strike and boycott. In line with his own quiet way of action, Chavez did not even tell his people he was fasting at first. It started in February 1968, amidst increasing talk of the need for violence both within his movement and among the fringe groups that supported him or sought his support. The strike had gone on for a year and a half, and his supporters were growing impatient with his philosophy of nonviolence. "Depressed, Chavez decided on the fast as a kind of penitence for the belligerence that had developed in his own union, and a commitment to nonviolence everywhere."[4] Chavez admitted he had come to the fast by way of Gandhi, but he also related to it from his Mexican Catholic penitential tradition. It was successful in quelling the growing violence within his own union and in galvanizing public and political support for his movement. At the mass celebrating its end, Chavez's address was read by another because of his weakness. In it he said: "It is my deepest belief that only by giving our lives do we find life. I am convinced that the truest act of courage, the strongest act of manliness, is to sacrifice ourselves for others in a totally nonviolent struggle for justice. To be a man is to suffer for others. God help us be men" (SSP, 195–96).

Cesar Chavez emerges from Matthiessen's book as a man for others, a leader of heroic proportions whose specific cause was hanging in the balance at the middle of 1969, the last events narrated in the book. At least, the two sides were in negotiation, which itself was "a gaping crack in the monolithic wall that the growers have shored up for four years, and that crack can only erode faster and faster" (*SSP,* 355). Matthiessen's book ends on a note of cautious optimism, the author like his subject, "refusing to give up hope for a new America" (*SSP,* 359).

In the Spirit of Crazy Horse

Fourteen years later, Matthiessen's tone turned considerably darker in his second book of social concern. *In the Spirit of Crazy Horse* (1983) is a 628-page jeremiad against the federal government's treatment of the American Indian as most recently manifested in its scandalous prosecution and conviction of Leonard Peltier for the murder of two FBI agents in June 1975. This arguably is Matthiessen's least read and most carefully read book. Libel suits totalling nearly $50 million were slapped on author and publisher in separate actions by FBI agent David Price and former South Dakota governor William Janklow shortly after the book's 1983 publication, causing Viking to pull the book off the shelves and sending the case's principals, their lawyers, and judges back to the massive tome with magnifying glasses. For nearly six years, the arguments swirled through state and district courts, at a cost of over $2 million to the defendants. In the end the courts exonerated Matthiessen, the final allegations of libel by Agent Price being dismissed by the U.S. Court of Appeals on 7 August 1989, and those by Janklow dismissed by the South Dakota Supreme Court in July 1990.

A letter from Matthiessen's lawyer, announcing the former decision on "one of the longest and most bitterly fought libel suits in U.S. history,"[5] arrived at the Matthiessen household coincidentally on the same day as my summer visit. Matthiessen emerged from his morning writing about 12:15 p.m., greeted me, and led me to the kitchen for lunch. Seeing the packet of mail on the counter, he leafed through it abstractedly, pulled out an envelope, and handed it to me with the comment, "You might be interested in this. It should be good news about the Crazy Horse book." Obviously he had already heard the court results by phone, which accounted somewhat for his lack of emotion. When I asked him about his subdued reaction, he said, yes, of course, he was happy, especially because of the implications of this decision for other writers, but that it had been a long process and the feeling was more relief than joy.

The court's decision, despite the narrowness of the libel issue with which it dealt, is a model of good literary criticism, not only sorting out Matthiessen's factual allegations from his opinions and both of these from those of others, but more important, interpreting all of the above in the larger context of the book's argument. Reading the decision makes one aware of just how careful Matthiessen had been in his reporting on the murders and how subtly he had built his case by means of the testimony of others. The court ruled that agent Price's complaint, in extracting statements out of context, "distorts the flavor of the book," and that "in its entirety, Crazy Horse focuses more on public institutions and social forces than it does on any public official." The court concluded that the sentiments expressed in the book are indeed debatable, and therefore, "We favor letting the debate continue."[6]

The court correctly interprets the book as focusing on public institutions and social forces more than on individuals. Without apology for his pro-Indian sympathies, Matthiessen solidifies and expands the indictment of the government's treatment of the American Indian initiated in such books as *Bury My Heart at Wounded Knee* and *Custer Died for Your Sins*. While the factual center of Matthiessen's book is the incident of 26 June 1975—an explosive act of violence on the Pine Ridge Reservation that left two FBI agents and one Indian dead—Matthiessen sees these events in the spirit of Crazy Horse, arguably the greatest war leader and symbol of Indian resistance to the cycle of violence, blandishments, and betrayal used by the U.S. government to seize Indian land. In order to establish a historical continuity between the events of the 1970s and the past, Matthiessen traces the interaction between white and red man in the Black Hills of South Dakota back to its beginnings in the late 1700s.

It is a story of mutual toleration turned into conflict as the white man encroached in increasing numbers upon hithertofore exclusively Indian territory, bringing along his plagues of alcohol and disease. The government, at times eager to avoid conflict, entered into a series of treaties with the Lakota and Dakota tribes (collectively the Sioux), treaties honored only until expediency or greed led to further appropriation. It is a story of treaties made and treaties abrogated, the latter usually sanctioned by the forced signature of whatever Indians were not in armed resistance. In 1876, for example, only eight years after the Indian had secured the Black Hills "in perpetuity," a new document of cancellation was forced upon Red Cloud, awarding the Black Hills to the white man in exchange for reservation land and rations.

Throughout the official process of continual aggrandizement of Indian land, the government systematically has rewarded Indian compliance and integration into white society, creating a divisiveness between traditionals and those who adapted. As Matthiessen says, "Among the Lakota, the grievous split between these factions (encouraged as part of the colonial strategy all over the world) dates back to the days when 'loafer' Indians

around the forts on the Bozeman Trail first got a taste of the white man's
liquor and molasses; when Spotted Tail and Red Cloud were flattered and
manipulated by trips to Washington; when Crazy Horse and Sitting Bull,
'resisting arrest,' were killed with the help of their own Indians, who served
the whites as Indian Agency police."[7] It is frightening to see contemporary
Indian events in the light of this history, especially if one assumes, as I had,
that the current government Indian policy is one of enlightened retribution
for the sins of the past. Matthiessen's book sees the present as a continua-
tion of the past, the same governmental dynamic of divide and conquer still
practiced. And now that the reservation land in the Black Hills area has
been discovered to have rich mineral deposits, it becomes expedient to ap-
propriate again that which was given back.

The bulk of the book is devoted to the tension and conflict within the Indian community and between the militant Indians of the American Indian
Movement (AIM) and U.S. government agencies. Matthiessen contends
(and the book is contentious) that the FBI has systematically harassed and
persecuted AIM and that the violence at Wounded Knee in 1973 and on
Pine Ridge in 1975 resulted from a concerted policy of neutralizing the political effectiveness of AIM. Behind this neutralization Matthiessen sees only
the dark motivations of racial prejudice and greed. The Indian activists too
often get in the way of the economic expansion which government and large
business view as desirable, whether that expansion involves the mining of
uranium or the building of dams for electric power.

Matthiessen lets the Indians speak for themselves, at too great a length
and too repetitiously for a readable book; and he culls the official documents relating to the government's prosecution of first Bob Robideau and
Dino Butler (both acquitted) and then Leonard Peltier (convicted and in
jail) for murder of the two FBI agents at Pine Ridge in June 1975. Both tri-
als are traced in detail, the book gradually focusing on Peltier, whom
Matthiessen believes to be innocent. The line of Matthiessen's argument—
while it subtly and massively builds Peltier's character by dint of the testimony of those who know him—is not to establish Peltier's innocence as
much as to establish the improper methods used to extradite him from Canada and then convict him of the crime. It is clear that the monumental effort
of interviewing behind this book, including the time spent building trust
among Indians wary of white reporters, was intended to result in a new trial
for Peltier, who is serving concomitant life prison terms. At the very least,
the book convinces the reader that Peltier deserves this, for he looks too
much like a convenient scapegoat in the light of the pattern of FBI and
prosecution tactics unearthed by Matthiessen.

Who actually killed the agents is another matter. Although Matthiessen finally gets around to constructing an alternate view of the crime, plausibly exonerating Peltier, such a scenario remains inconclusive because no killer is ever named, by Matthiessen, Peltier, or anybody else who was there. For whatever reason—Indian honor, inscrutable belief that this execution was within the context of war—Peltier and the other principals Matthiessen talked to seem less than candid in their disclosures. Matthiessen would like us to believe that they really don't know who the executioner was or that they are strong enough to resist squealing just to save themselves, but their lack of frankness leaves lingering doubts in the reader's mind. In apparent recognition of this inconclusiveness, Matthiessen suggests that "talk of guilt or innocence in the inevitable shoot-out seemed beside the point" (*SCH,* 478). Perhaps in a "shoot-out" Matthiessen would be right because of the mutually provocative climate of violence, but forensic evidence mentioned in the book seemed to indicate an execution of wounded men at close range.[8] In such a case, guilt or innocence could never be beside the point.

Matthiessen's position is further weakened by his admitted predisposition of sympathy with the convicted man and his cause. At times, it seems the overwhelming mountain of testimony has been heaped more as a barrier than a window to truth. More is not necessarily better, especially when a number of the sources themselves have backgrounds clouded by violence, alcohol, and drug abuse. The climate of criminality that Matthiessen shows to surround the AIM group itself surely must bear some responsibility for the violence that ensued. Even the words of AIM leaders, quoted at length by Matthiessen, have a hardened coldness to violence in general and to the murders in particular.

It is true that Matthiessen gives the devil his due in interviewing by phone Agent Price, but the interview comes strategically late in the book, well after Matthiessen has set all his opinions like rock, and it is just one voice from the other side. Had Matthiessen early on talked to the FBI, the Bureau of Indian Affairs, and the Indian leaders who oppose AIM, one would feel more confident, given the documented judicial recognition of FBI abuses in this case, in believing the book's suggestions of collusion and persecution of the militant Indians. Of course, they might well not have co-operated anyway, given the author's bias. And yet, why didn't Matthiessen talk to some of the supporters of the tribal council and its elected and reelected leader, Richard Wilson, the starkest villain of the book? Matthiessen, despite his well-documented recitation of Wilson's outrageous abuses of power, never fully confronts Wilson's popularity on Pine Ridge.

All this is not to say that Matthiessen's polemic about "the government's remorseless attitude toward militant Indians," who live in the spirit of Crazy Horse defending their traditional rights, is not convincing. *In the Spirit of Crazy Horse* is enormously persuasive, but it remains a polemic for all that. Matthiessen's first piece of writing for the *New Yorker* was an "Annals of Crime" contribution about a French murder case; his prose in *Crazy Horse* returns to that of the objective crime reporter. Only here, the testimony he takes is all one-sided, and he lets his witnesses speak too uninterruptedly and too long. *In the Spirit of Crazy Horse* ultimately is a practical book, lacking the poetry and shaping imagination of Matthiessen's better nonfiction. One hopes, now that the legal impediments have been cleared to its publication, that it may rekindle the kind of debate the court thought beneficial to the public good. Perhaps it will also garner further support for a deserved new trial for Leonard Peltier, who seems unjustly incarcerated, and incite public resistance to any further government trespassing on Indian lands and ways.

Indian Country

Indian Country (1984) continues the argument for the revitalization of traditional Indian ways and the protection of Indian territory in twelve different and unconnected contexts, from the Chumash defense of the sacred Point Conception, California, to the Miccosukee efforts to reclaim its Everglades homeland in Florida. The book collects previously published articles detailing Matthiessen's visits to Indian settlements across the country, each chapter chronicling a particular problem—often with environmental, political, and historic significance—for a particular tribe. Take the Hopi, for example, where the old ways have been preserved in a purer state than among any other Indian tribe, and to whom "Indians of North America now look for spiritual guidance."[9] Since the leaders of the traditional villages had never signed a treaty with the U.S. government, it was significant when the Hopi were asked to accept $5 million, through negotiations worked out by a lawyer retained by the Hopi Tribal Council, in recompense for lands taken from them. At first blush this seems like the act of a contrite government making retribution for past sins. It may even seem like reasonable recompense until we learn the price comes out to between sixty-two cents and two dollars an acre, a figure based on the price of land in the 1900s when the land was taken, which worked out to less than one thousand dollars per Hopi, a sum that shrinks even more in comparison with the attorney's $500,000 fee. Even so, some payment for the past might be thought better than nothing. The Hopi Tribal Council, which according to Matthiessen is a prospering bureaucracy that depends primarily upon its income from mineral leases, tried to persuade the Hopi people of this sentiment. What the Hopi Tribal Council did not say was that the acceptance of such recompense would clear the way for further leasing of land to large energy interests, interests represented for over fifteen years by the firm of the same lawyer who had been hired by the council.

In reading *Indian Country,* one perceives there is money to be made on Indian issues by Indians and others, and this money greases bureaucratic wheels and sets Indian against Indian, with the controlling Indians of the Tribal Councils usually prospering and the traditional Indians who resist acculturation into white society becoming more isolated and diminished. Usually what happens is that the whole tribe is compromised by the divisiveness, allowing the force of money and manipulation (the Hopi Council held the vote on the day of the traditional Basket Dance, effectively excluding the opposition) to carry the day.

While one may feel uneasy about the conspiratorial implications of Matthiessen's portrait of the three-pronged front of government agencies (including the Bureau of Indian Affairs), business interests ("multinational concerns"), and tribal councils, it is hard to deny the mutuality of their interests and the concertedness of their actions on many controversial issues. In example after example, the Indians who run the tribal councils prosper through cooperation with government and business, happy to augment their own income and that of their underlings. Their lawyers prosper through government settlements, collecting hefty percentages of amounts that look large until one realizes the vast amounts of land being recompensed and their actual value. The U.S. and local governments are delighted to clear away Indian claims for land illegally taken, surgically removing an ugly scar on the body politic, and eliminating the need to deal further with Indian land problems. And the corporations, whoever they are, Kerr-McGee, Pacific Gas & Electric, or Union Carbide, are free to exploit the valuable resources of the earth whatever the environmental consequences.

The latter have always been a concern of Matthiessen's, and he details an astonishing amount of pollution and environmental damage by many of the corporations that operate in Indian country. Uranium, coal, and oil drilling leads to water depletion, contamination, and radiation dangers in the Black Hills. Defoliation and logging by lumber companies in the Siskiyou Mountains of Northern California poison the streams and wildlife. The desire to generate unneeded electric power and more jobs in Tennessee leads to the most egregious and, to my mind, reprehensible example of environmental outrage cited by Matthiessen in the book, not to mention the affront to

Indian sensibilities because of the special religious significance of the area. The Tellico Dam proposal caused national debate, but in the end:

A beautiful river known affectionately throughout the state as the "Little T" has been stopped up like a clogged pork barrel to create a muddy artificial lake, and silted beneath this superfluous lake will lie not only the drowned homesteads of hundreds of defenseless people but also sixteen thousand acres of some of the richest river-bottom farmland in the United States, and an historical treasure perhaps as important as all these other losses put together: the hundreds of archeological sites in the Little Tennessee Valley include not only ancient mounds but the buried ruins of the Seven Towns that two centuries ago were the sacred center of the Cherokee Nation. (*IC*, 109)

Matthiessen is at his best when writing about the environment. He knows it better than he knows Indians, and his outrage in this book at the abuse of both is supported by example after example. In that sense, the book raises our consciousness on both fronts simultaneously.

Each chapter of *Indian Country* takes Matthiessen to a different tribe in a different part of the country with roughly the same problems: intertribal conflict between traditionals and nontraditionals; pressures from large economic interests, in cooperation with government agencies, either to use more Indian territory or to further abuse the territory already appropriated; an increasingly threatened quality of life from environmental destruction; and hostility from local and state law enforcement bodies. Whether it's the Cherokee and the Tellico Dam or the Mohawk and the near-violent raid by N.Y. State Police or the Hopi and the stripping of sacred mountains, the story is one of a people once in harmony with nature, clinging to vestiges of this heritage so badly needed by our society at large, now driven to some of the country's most undesirable territories, made dependent upon a white society for money, food, alcohol, and religion, and divided by varying degrees of acculturation into two factions. It is a situation made all the more painful and complicated by the government's institution of a tribal governing system which lends itself to gross abuses of violence and greed.

The underlying tragedies of Matthiessen's picture are many. For the Indians, life is not good on the reservations, where illiteracy, alcoholism, unemployment, and violence abound. Only in pockets of Indian life, usually the secluded traditionalist pockets like the Hopi mesas, does the old oneness with nature survive. For our larger society, the tragedy is that the original Indian vision of respect for nature and sharing of its treasures, which was offered by the country's first inhabitants to its European visitors, has been ignored, even trashed. This vision cannot be expressed any better than by Mohawk chief Tom Porter: "The land wasn't given to us as a commodity but entrusted to us; we are its custodians, you might say, so that our children will have a place to put their little feet upon this earth. The Creator still sees the native people as custodians of this land; we think so, too. It is our *duty* to take care of it" (*IC,* 161–62).

The root of the conflict between the Indian vision and what has become the American vision can be seen as the difference between a Lockean and a Rousseauvian vision of man, a society governed by economics or one governed by anthropology, an ultimate allegiance to money and its ability to improve the quality of life or to the sacred and its ability to transform life at whatever stage of "development" it has reached. Matthiessen is a Rousseauvian, believing that man in his traditional communities had a wisdom and a oneness with the natural world that is more valuable than all the inventions, refinements, and political structures that civilization has brought.

Even an ambiguous and little visited ancient holy place like Doctor Rock, to which Matthiessen journeys in "The High Country," is revered by his Indian guide, John Trull, who admits he does not understand the old medicine rites performed there. And, when Matthiessen goes back to the place months later and encounters a lone old Indian on the same purpose, the Indian admits he has never been there before and does not quite know why he is going there now. For Matthiessen and for the Indian, however, there is something valuable, something sacred to which explanations are superfluous.

In the midst of *Indian Country*'s mostly positive and unremarkable reviews, Peter Nabokov's "Return to the Native" stands out by its formidable and cogent criticism. Nabokov, who has written on Indians himself, criticizes Matthiessen for being too monolithic in his picture of what it means to be Indian, blurring real differences from tribe to tribe, and obscuring the many variations between the poles of "traditional" and "nontraditional" within tribes. Where Matthiessen sees convergence of Indian ways, Nabokov sees diversity; where Matthiessen praises Indian unity based upon traditional beliefs, Nabokov praises the flexibility and adaptability of particular tribes, pointing out that even "old" beliefs like the Mohawks' that Matthiessen esteems are a synthesis of "Quaker ethics and selected rites from the older Iroquois ceremonial cycle."[10] Nabokov's reservations are grave enough and the added references he cites are relevant enough that his review should be read along with *Indian Country*. Its most serious charge, that Matthiessen's portrait of Indian life is a stereotype, perpetuating "the oldest images that whites have used to turn the Indians into symbols of their own deepest longings," is worth mulling over (Nabokov, 45). Nabokov's judgment, however, seems based more on one or two passages of Matthiessen's generalizations than on the texture of the entire book, which is drawn from twelve different Indian cultures and Matthiessen's firsthand visitations. If Matthiessen's sympathy has been elicited for traditional elements within each of these Indian cultures, he has demonstrated the basis for such sympathy in the particulars of each chapter. If a stereotype of traditional Indian ways emerges from the book, it comes from individual portraits. Nabokov's review implies that Matthiessen has not been empirical in his investigations, claiming that his "loyalties and evocations seem inherited from the earlier writers and approaches . . ." (Nabokov, 44); but, in fact, Matthiessen is short on generalities and long on particulars in the book. His traditional Indians all have names, histories, and the complexities of men and women who know they have lost something that may be only partly recoverable. Matthiessen never stints quirky details or unromantic realities in favor of pious platitudes or glimmering visions of the noble savage. If anything, most readers would probably prefer *more* reflection on how traditional Indian practices might be a leavening element in the civilization that surrounds it and needs it so badly.

Men's Lives

In his fourth book of advocacy, Matthiessen returns from his travels in Indian country to write about an area and a people he knows best, the Long Island fishermen. "It's not fish ye're buyin, it's men's lives," wrote Sir Walter Scott; Matthiessen's title indicates that it's not about fishing that we will be reading, but about men's lives, or at least about that inextricable union of work and identity that obtains for people who love what they do for a living. Since the baymen of Long Island's South Fork are threatened by diminishing catches of fish as well as by the shortsighted legislation of state government, *Men's Lives* (1986), like the other books in this chapter, articulates the cause of the voiceless. It is a tribute to a passing way of life, an elegy, an appreciation. This time, however, Matthiessen writes from the perspective of both participant and observer; for in 1953–56 he made his living fishing commercially with the Lesters, Edwards, and Havens, all families who had seined the Long Island waters for generations.

Regardless of his sympathies for Chavez, Peltier, and the traditional Indians, Matthiessen was always a guest-writer, living among them for the reporting. Here Matthiessen's voice has more inner authority, for he has paid his dues as a member of the haul-seine crews, dredged for scallops and clams, and run his own charter boat operation. In fact, there is quite a bit of autobiography in the book, as Matthiessen mentions his early fishing with his father off nearby Montauk Point, having spent most of his first fifteen summers on Fishers Island, which lies only eight miles northeast of Long Island. In 1953, after his stint in Paris, Matthiessen moved to the South Fork because, he says, he "was unsuited to urban work and . . . sought a leaner way of life outdoors" (*ML,* 56). He enjoyed the fishing and the balance it gave to his writing life, feeling accepted by the men for whom this was a heritage as well as a job. "Associated with unprivileged men," he says, "doing hard labor with my hands, I felt more free, less malcontent, than at any time in all my life" ("NY," 70). After three years of fishing, Matthiessen began the travels for which he would become famous, but he returned to the area often, buying a house in 1960 and making Sagaponack his permanent home.

The book begins with a history of the area and the origins of its fishing industry among colonists and Indians, tracing this fishing history up until the 1950s. The second part deals with Matthiessen's firsthand experiences as a haul-seiner, clammer, and charter-boat captain. The final third of the book discusses the threatened state of the occupation in 1986, its virtual destruction because of the governmental ban on bass fishing, and the decline of the scallop harvest. Matthiessen focuses throughout on the people and their vanishing way of life. He tells of the various Uncle Freds, Cap'n Bills, and Haven boys, lavishing details about their financial conditions, mannerisms, superstitions, family history, and devotion to fishing. Although after a while I could not and, indeed, did not care to keep all the individuals apart, I knew the essential spirit of the Long Island fisherman—salty, dogged, and committed to a life far removed from the workaday world of most people. The men love what they do. The sad thing is that the old times are vanishing, and the younger generations, while still imbued with the same attachments to the sea and the fishing, can no longer make ends meet. New government regulations, limiting the size of the striped-bass catch, then prohibiting it altogether, stripped away one of the few remaining profitable aspects of the seine fishery. Even those flexible enough to alternate trap fishing and shellfish harvesting with their seining are unable to make enough money to support families.

As a strong and eloquent advocate for the baymen, Matthiessen makes the reader aware of the complexity of environmental, economic, political, and personal issues involved. New York's Department of Environmental Conservation chooses to ban the seine fishermen from taking the stripers instead of attacking the industrial pollution that affects the spawning grounds of these fish. Sport fishermen form a convenient alliance with these alleged environmentalists, of course, protecting their own hobby, which the author notes sometimes becomes a sideline commercial venture. Politicians eager to make reputations out of headline issues join the bandwagon of "environmental protection," while ignoring the paucity of hard scientific data about the status of the very species, in this case the striped bass, they are supposedly protecting. It is a painful situation, made more so by the lesson of political insensitivity to people's rights and ways of life when these people don't have sufficient numbers or power to exert political influence.

The happier theme of the book is that of the baymen themselves, hardy and tough, independent and indomitable. Their unique life is Thoreauvian in its simplicity, self-determination, and hierarchy of values, which puts style of work and life ahead of money, social pressure, status, or other factors. They speak in their own words to us, thanks to Matthiessen's excellent ear and patient recording. William Havens complains about the ignorance of the beachgoers who decry the fish left to die from the seiner's nets: "Anyways, why don't they know it don't do no good to throw most of them fish back? It ain't the haul-seiners' fault nobody wants 'em! Last week my men here shipped 309 pounds of bluefish. Know what we got back, after payin the shippin? Eleven-fifty! Eleven dollars and fifty cents for three hundred and nine pounds of good *bluefish!* Does that seem fair to you?" (*ML*, 285–86). Matthiessen does not hide his sympathy, noting that a friend had just spent $11.50 in a nearby restaurant for a bluefish dinner.

Despite all the problems with the markets and the scarcity, the old-timers know that if the government would just leave them alone everything would be all right. They know scarcity, for they have lived with it for years, but they also know that plenty eventually follows. As Cap'n Bill said about the bass that had practically disappeared, "one of these days they'll be comin in thick as they ever was" (*ML*, 303). And sure enough, he was right, for in 1985 the bass returned in large numbers. As Matthiessen reports in his epilogue, however, that resurgence was not enough to prevent the complete New York prohibition against catching this "endangered" bass the following year.

Matthiessen's writing is factual, chiseled, and, as always, informed by the terminology and idioms of his subject matter. His style, somewhat mechanical and driven perhaps by the duties of conscience in the Chavez and Indian books, breathes freely again. His descriptions are chaste: "We went down to Napeague just as the sun came up on a calm wintry sea. In this season whales are sometimes seen from shore, and the white flash of diving gannets, harassing the fish schools heading south, but this morning the sea was entirely empty, a gray waste extending without a mark to the horizon. The clouds of bait had disappeared, and the bird legions; the rush of storm seas had subsided to a soft whisper in the shining shallows. On the tide line were thin windrows of dead sand fleas, killed by the first frost of coming winter" (*ML,* 286). Matthiessen is as celebratory of the ocean's moods and the essential poetry of the common man as that other resident of Long Island, Walt Whitman, ever was. Matthiessen's praise, however, is always quieter, the praise of close observation rather than incantation.

Men's Lives, despite its advocacy of the fisherman's lifestyle and its defense of his freedom to ply it in the face of government restrictions, is lighter, less obsessed than Matthiessen's other socially conscious books. It does not seem, as Peter Nabokov correctly observed about the Indian books, "a burden of conscience" to Matthiessen. The author's own energies so blend with those of the people and the surroundings he writes about that the book moves with a natural grace and power. Indeed, *Men's Lives* possesses a factual lyricism and personal passion that put it among Matthiessen's best nonfiction.

Chapter Seven

Experimental Novelist: The Precedence of Fiction

Far Tortuga

Experiential Base

Far Tortuga (1975) is at once Matthiessen's most ambitious novel and his most definitive commitment to the vocation of novelist as a higher calling than that of chronicler. Like most of his writing, it is based upon a personal experience, in this case, a 1967 voyage aboard the schooner *Lydia E. Wilson,* which left Grand Cayman in April to search for the green sea turtle in the cays of the western Caribbean. Since the trip was financed by the *New Yorker,* Matthiessen wrote a report of it ("To the Miskito Bank," 28 October 1967) for the magazine, although—as mentioned in chapter 4—he withheld from the piece what he considered to be the best material. Afraid to disturb his deepest impressions from the trip, Matthiessen wrote the *New Yorker* account quickly and straightforwardly. In it he tells us that he slept on deck partly because it allowed him to listen to the conversations of the crew directly below, but he does not say, except for a few exchanges, what those conversations were. He merely summarizes: "The men spoke of old turtlers and turtle boats, of great storms on the Miskito Bank, of the barracuda and poisonous jacks that are caught off the Six-Mile Beach, and of the witchcraft called obeah, come to the Caymans from Jamaica."[1] One would be hard pressed to come up with a better one-sentence summary of most of *Far Tortuga,* for the novel is practically all conversation, a great deal of it about these very subjects, and all of it in the inflections of the individual crew members.

In the typical way of Matthiessen's nonfiction, the *New Yorker* piece is informative about the history of turtling, the dwindling number of green turtles, their shifting and narrowing habitats, and the turtle's amazing feats of navigation. And we get a sense of the ship's captain, Cadian Ebanks, its crew, mostly Caymanians except for two men from Honduras, and what it's like to sail on an old schooner that has been adapted to the modern world

by the addition of a diesel engine (although the job was done so quickly that
the helmsman's vision is completely blocked by the deckhouse). Many of
the above details of the journey make their way into the novel. Most notably
Captain Cadian Ebanks and most of his crew are models for Captain Raib
Avers and his men. Two of the men's names are not even changed, Speedy
and Brown, and their descriptions in the article are consistent with their
roles in the novel. The first mate in both versions confounds the captain by
setting the turtle nets too far away from the reef and still catching turtles.
Cadian Ebanks curses fate and his men and unaccountably breaks into a
wave of laughter, actions that become characteristic of Captain Raib. Captain Ebanks's temperament, his love for the sea and for his profession, and
his dissatisfaction with the changing times all clearly help mold his counterpart in the novel. When Ebanks hooks up for trolling some flying fish that
jumped aboard the boat during the night, he says, "You fly too high, darlin'
. . . and you come to a crahsh lahndin'" ("Miskito," 150), almost the same
words Avers will use in the novel. One night on a particularly rough sea with
a wind that was no longer merely stiff but "something ominous,"
Matthiessen kept watch with Captain Cadie, talking "for hours before
dawn" ("Miskito," 159). Again, however, like the conversations of the crew
that he overheard from his on-deck sleeping place, this talk goes unreported
in the article. Evidently, since the voices of these men become so important
in the novel, these conversations were some of the "best material" that
Matthiessen consciously withheld from his report.

Unlike the novel, the article has no conclusion and no thematic unity. We
feel something for the green turtle and we understand what it's like for the
men who have made their livelihood out of hunting them, but that is all.
The account lacks soul. Matthiessen leaves the ship before the journey is
complete, having all along made tentative provisions to go home by way of
Nicaragua when the *Wilson* docks there. As in his trip to the South American wilderness, Matthiessen's personal experience goes only so far. Just as he
did not visit the remote Indian tribe or search for the Inca ruins in *The Cloud
Forest*, so in "To the Miskito Bank" he is content with only half of an un-
eventful turtling voyage. Since he had waited over two years to make the
trip, Matthiessen's motivation in going ashore is puzzling, and he does not
comment on it in the essay. Had he had enough of the discomforts of the
Wilson? Or did he have a foreboding about this ill-equipped and blindly
steered ship? When I put these questions to Matthiessen, his answer was:
"Well, the ship was a terrible old ship. But they were awfully good sailors.
No, it wasn't that. I was just kinda worn out. It was very rough. The seas
were uncomfortable, really terrible. But mainly, I'd been on the ship about

twelve days, and I got what I wanted. I really felt I got what I expected to find there." As I had suspected, Matthiessen's imagination had been fired, and he needed no more material. He wanted to return in order to start writing, to get the piece for the *New Yorker* out of the way, and then to launch into the novel that would take him eight more years to finish, the novel that would become his greatest achievement as a writer.

Artistic Transformation

The form of *Far Tortuga* has more affinity with Matthiessen's early novels than with its immediate predecessor, *At Play in the Fields of the Lord,* which is fairly conventional in its thick sinewy realism, its delving into character motivation, and its lush description. As in the earlier books, Matthiessen takes the "less is more" narrative tack in his fifth novel. *Partisans,* in particular, experimented with form, suppressing narrative commentary and telling much of its story through dialogue. Nothing, however, in *Partisans* nor in any of his previous books could prepare the reader for the stylistic daring of *Far Tortuga.* If the reviewers agree on anything, it is that Matthiessen takes a stylistic leap of faith with this book, faith in his vision of what form his subject called for. They speak of "the originality of its form," "the curious quality of the book's narrative style," "its impressionist form," and judge the results variously as a "stylistic tour de force," a "virtuoso novel" in which "Matthiessen's art prevails," a "magnificent performance," a "difficult yet successful undertaking," an "unrelieved bore," and "a work of brilliance."[2]

The stylistic uniqueness of the book derives from its preponderance of dialogue over narration. In a short interview about the novel's craft, Matthiessen admits that he modeled the physical format of the book on "the screenplay, even though the person speaking is not identified directly, and the camera directions are replaced by descriptive writing."[3] Not identifying the speaker makes considerable demands on the reader, and even Matthiessen in the interview admits that one voice is nearly indistinguishable from another in the early going; he claims, however, that by the time it's important for the reader to know precisely who is speaking, the speaker will be recognized "by the idiosyncrasies of speech" and "by his small obsessions" ("Craft," 81). He is right. As demanding as the book is, it clarifies as it progresses. In fact, the very process by which the cacophony of voices grows more distinct and less a common wail of woe derives from the natural dynamic of differentiation that occurs to a group of men isolated through the confinement of a ship's journey. The refrains of Byrum and Speedy and

Brown become more distinguishable as they are repeated and as they reflect growing conflict aboard the ship. As the journey increases in hardship, bad luck, and danger, the voices become even more separate, for men act differently under pressure and the small fissures that had opened earlier in the voyage have widened to chasms by the novel's end.

Also contributing to the stylistic singularity of the book are its typographic format and what reviewers have called its impressionist technique. The former involves use of considerable white space, such that paragraphs, sentences, and sometimes words are given ample breathing room, to the extent that a strategic phrase or word occasionally occupies an entire page. Chapter 14, for example, begins with the word, "Midnight." Three spaces below, we read, "Low murmuring. A cough."[4] Then a sectional graphic, followed by "One A.M." and another sectional graphic. The sectional graphics are circles, variously shaded to suggest the phases of the sun. Other artwork is used on occasion for important events such as the death of characters and the shipwreck itself, and for natural phenomena like the horizon on a clear day or the evening star. A meticulous drawing of the ship itself from different angles gives the reader a clear picture of the stage of the drama. In the original hardcover edition, even a map of the western Caribbean is added. All this "rigging" helps the reader maintain perspective, eliminating the need for elaborate description while enforcing the realistic effect of the tale.

It also contributes to Matthiessen's intention of creating a physical object that mirrors in its sensual effects the experience of the trip. He says, "I attempted using white space to achieve resonance, to make the reader receive things intuitively, hear the silence in the wind, for instance, that is a constant presence in the book" ("Craft," 80). Of course, not every writer has a publisher as cooperative as Matthiessen's, although a couple of the author's remarks hint that the battles over such matters must have been bloody. In acknowledging his editor, Joe Fox, Matthiessen writes, "we have been through hell together" (*FT,* Acknowledgments). And in the *Paris Review* interview, he refers to "the mechanical problems of these spaces in terms of the printed page, and in the end I had to compromise on the white-space idea" ("Craft," 80). Compromise or not, Matthiessen has wrought a book that breathes and sighs, more palpable than any novel I have read.

The notion that Matthiessen's style is impressionist derives from James Dickey's dust-jacket prediction that the novel "will certainly point the way that the English-speaking sensibility must and should go, . . . the way of passionate impressionism." For one thing, the style of the book is not passionate at all. As Thomas Edwards points out, it is a "spare and sober [book], sympathetically respectful of its subjects but very cool."[5] The novel, indeed, is chiseled and unemotional, presenting the natural reality and allowing the emotional effect of that reality to register in the reader. As for the impressionism, the other reviewers have echoed Dickey's label, but I think the description and prediction mislead. Again, Edwards's qualification helps: "[T]his 'impressionistic' method surely wouldn't work for a different kind of material. The blank spaces on the page create and sustain a slow regularity of tempo, isolating utterance in the midst of emptiness, that beautifully suits an elegiac story about the sea but would seem pretentiously arty in most other connections" (Edwards, 35). Actually Matthiessen's style is more minimalist than impressionist. All is cut back in the way of description, and metaphor is virtually eliminated. Matthiessen himself acknowledges that the sole exception to the latter is the simile for an island, "like a memory in the ocean emptiness" ("Craft," 82). While there are certainly other metaphors that occur to describe actions, such as the boats "banging across the wind in white explosions" (*FT*, 173), even these are kept to a minimum in order to capture the elemental nature of the experience being presented. We focus on the small world of the *Lillias Eden* and the actions of her men as they ply their turtling trade on "de bleak ocean" under a burning sun and buffeted by strong winds.

By his literalness and reductionism, Matthiessen wants the reader to concentrate on the stark, unromanticized realities of the voyage. The sun and wind and starry darkness are mentioned so insistently because they are the context of any other experience on such a trip:

A cool night wind, and stars.
In the bows, a clank of chain and shriek of ratchet; a storm lamp shudders in the galley.
Silhouettes on the night sky.
Over the engine hatch, the yellow bulb rolls with the ship, shifting the shadows. Raib is crouched over the hole, hands on knees, peering below; his voice is muted, in respect for darkness. (*FT*, 123)

The sentences are strung out in careful bareness, focusing attention on the present experience. Matthiessen's voice is muted, like Raib's, in respect for the darkness and for every other immediate reality. The staccato sentences create a kind of hushed reverence, investing each moment with a sacred intensity. Matthiessen admits that his study of Zen may have "contributed to a need for spareness, the presentation of a coffee cup, a cockroach, with a minimum of literary adornment. Zen training helps one to see in a fresh way . . . and I suppose I am trying to present things directly, let objects and

actions speak for themselves . . ." ("Craft," 80). This unadorned directness
is effective. Not only does it bring the reader face to face with the discrete
experiences of the trip, but it also counterpoints nicely with the musical
sway of the Caribbean dialects. In the following excerpt, Captain Raib has
just sent out a catboat on a wild sea to pick up the remaining turtle nets.

> The men on deck watch their shipmates disappear. They do not speak for a long
> time. Raib picks up a torn net and begins to mend it, but soon his hands stop; he
> gazes out to sea.
> Dat ocean look so *old* in de mornin time.
> He frowns at the uneasy faces.
> You see de way Vemon smile dere, Speedy? What de hell he *smilin* at? (*shakes his
> head*) Dat one thing I got to say about old Vemon—dat fool surprise you. I knowed
> him since we was children, and every time I think I know de kind of a fool he is, he
> turn around and give me a surprise.
> Vemon ain't no fool. No, mon. He just *play* de fool, cause for him, dass de way
> life go de best. (*FT,* 229)

Throughout the novel the two languages of narration and dialogue play
against each other, the one flat and staccato, the other highly inflected and
richly rhetorical, the language of fact and the language of feeling.

If the interplay between the impersonal narrative voice and the personal
speaking voice simply created rhythmic and melodic variety, it would be a
clever and useful device. Matthiessen's artistry in the styling of the book,
however, is evident when we realize that these two voices reflect the underlying conflict of the novel, that between the personal and the impersonal, between desire and fate. Furthermore, the variety of individual inflections
within the dialogue reflect the other interpersonal conflicts of the story. The
voyage is conceived of in as many different ways as there are individuals on
board, but Captain Raib promises to make these individuals into a crew before the journey's end. "Dey ain't much," he says, "but I intendin to make
turtlers out of dem" (*FT,* 39). Conflict exists, then, not only among the
men, and between their collective individualism and Raib's effort to mold
them into a unit, but overarchingly between the ship of human desire and
the reefs of time, nature, and chance.

The book's style mirrors and reinforces these conflicts. The impersonal
stark power of the narration represents these impersonal forces, and the
voices of the crew and their captain express the varieties of human desire
and human ingenuity as they confront these forces. Even in the brief excerpt
above, one can see these contrasts. In the narrative paragraph, each of the

five statements is written in the same order, subject-verb-object. The next narrative sentence is the same. One senses in the structural repetitiveness and in the words themselves the inevitability of the action described. A catboat had to go out on a very dangerous sea to pick up the remaining turtle nets; the captain and remaining crew can do nothing to help. The first line of dialogue, Raib's comment, "Dat ocean look so *old* in de mornin time," brings us into the world of subjectivity and conflict. The verb describes an impression, one that is given emphasis and inflection with the italics on "old," and one that is not shared by the crew. In fact, his respect for the sea and its oldness and for the oldness of man's coping with the sea is something Raib continually and futilely tries to instill in his crew. The next line of narration hints of the crew's failure to grasp the depths that Raib wants them to, for they are simply uneasy over the immediate situation—fearing for the catboat's and their own safety—not out of any understanding of the ocean. The conflicts, then, between Raib and the men and between the human collective and the sea are seen in this microcosm of lines. Raib's next comment is addressed to Speedy, whom he respects more than the others in the crew, and it also betrays his grudging affection for the buffoonish Vemon. Raib, in enlisting Vemon for the trip and throwing away Vemon's rum bottle, thinks he can reform even the confirmed alcoholic. He sees Vemon as being totally unregenerate, however, and himself as being totally salvific. Speedy's reply shows his characteristic respect and understanding of all the crew, something Raib lacks. Speedy's comment is also prophetic in that Vemon leaves the ship at Bragman's Bluff and thus avoids the ensuing catastrophe. Speedy is right about him: "He just *play* de fool, cause for him dass de way life go de best" (*FT*, 229).

Contrasts in language, then, both among the crew's and the captain's colorful utterances and between these utterances and the bare narration operate symbolically as well as musically. The men's voices are full of desire, full of individuality, full of emotion. The narrative voice is cold and impersonal. The success of the journey will depend on how these voices of desire, both collectively and individually, deal with the impersonal forces of the changing times, elemental nature, and unpredictable fortune.

Speculative Implications

Peter Matthiessen's stories are too deeply planted in character and dialogue for him to be labeled a novelist of ideas. Yet, as we have seen, there are ideas in all his earlier novels. And *Far Tortuga,* a story about a ship's tragic expedition, could hardly leave port without a cargo of thought. As Paul

Gray in his *Time* review put it, "Literary sea voyages often carry a heavy ballast of allegory. The potential, after all, is readymade; it requires no great leap of imagination to see a ship as a tiny world adrift in eternity." Gray goes on, however, to say that *Far Tortuga* "shuns such metaphysics in favor of hard surfaces."[6] I would agree that the book's course is guided more by its "hard surfaces" than by a metaphysical overview, and yet I would argue that a definite structure of thought evolves from these surfaces. After all, this is no ordinary ship, but the *Eden,* a name Matthiessen decided to use instead of the actual ship of his own expedition, the *Lydia E. Wilson.* And while there is a real Misteriosa Bank, Matthiessen obviously appropriates the name for the reefs upon which the *Eden* eventually founders on account of its symbolic connotation. What is, in fact, impressive about the book's construction is that meaning arises from the "hard surfaces" of reality, instead of being imposed upon these surfaces in an allegorical manner. It is not surprising that the names of Melville and Conrad came up in a number of reviews since both of them have written great novels of the sea with the same convincing elements of reality that Matthiessen exhibits here. Like theirs, Matthiessen's reality also has a visionary dimension. His vision has to do with the conflicts mentioned at the end of the previous section. How does man deal with our changing modern world, our unchanging natural world, and the vagaries of chance?

"De Modern Time"   A persistent motif of the novel is that times are changing, the old ways falling sadly to the new. The very stage of the entire book's drama, the *Lillias Eden,* epitomizes the changing times. The ship, one of the fastest schooners plying the Caribbean waters, patterned after the old Gloucester vessels in its original construction from Cayman mahogany, has undergone the addition of twin diesel engines and the shortening of her masts. Since Captain Raib ran out of money and the turtle season was slipping away, the job had to be curtailed before the steering wheel could be relocated. Consequently the helmsman now has no view of the ship's path, looking directly into the back of the deckhouse, which had to be elevated to make room for the engines. The result is a symbol of the modern world, where progress—in the form of an engine—is sought at the expense of vision. Byrum, when he sees the changes, shakes his head, "Mon! I never think she come home from Honduras lookin poor as dat!" Speedy, who is from Honduras and understands that change is everywhere, replies with what becomes his familiar refrain, "You in de modern time, mon: sailin boat a thing of de past." Byrum insists that this is a change for the worse, suggesting that the *Eden* looks "like a goddom *Jamaica* boat" (*FT,* 17). Jamaica, throughout the crew's conversations, is a sign of all that is decadent and unwelcome in the modern world. Jamaicans encountered at sea are "rascally-lookin people—dey no good, mon" (*FT,* 190). Later, it will be Jamaican egg-hunters, high on weed, who precipitate the *Eden*'s disaster.

Captain Raib rails out against the modern times at every opportunity, his voice becoming a refrain of regret and resistance.[7] It is true that he is responsible for the mechanical adaptation of the *Eden,* but he did so only in order to survive the competition for the dwindling catch of turtle. He laments the wanton killing of all wildlife that has diminished the days of abundance: "Dey killed off de seals just like dey killin off green turtle, and de crocodiles before dem. De snipes is gone now. Ain't no iguana left up at Northwest. Mahogany, logwood, fustic—all dat gone now! Dey cuttin it all away!" (*FT,* 145). Raib is known for his caustic tongue, and he tells his crew openly and bitterly that they are part of the problem. They are the modern world in all of its undisciplined, lazy, untrained, and irreverent ways. Each one of the crew confirms this judgment by his behavior, the lone exception being Speedy, who also is the only one Raib holds any hope for.

The most extreme example of this modern way is Brown, the engineer who stays to himself, boasts about his necrophilia, steals Captain Andrew's knife, and later betrays the entire crew. Speedy, who is blessed with the gift of understanding, explains the desperateness of a character like Brown as a result of the desperate quality of life in many places: "What Brownie mean—well, in all dese countries now, we gettin quite a problem. Malaria got to be a thing of de past, all dem old kind sickness dere, so we got to de place where *nobody* dyin, and dey ain't enough of anything to go around. Den people start actin like wild animals. La Violencia. No work, no money, nothin. So all dey carin about is pussy, cause dat all dey got" (*FT,* 308). Raib cannot compromise with such modernity, no matter what the consequence. He despises Captain Desmond Eden, his supposed half-brother, who perverts the role of captain by his mercenary opportunism and personal dissipation, running refugees to islands in pretense that they are the United States. Desmond associates freely with the Jamaicans that Raib will have nothing to do with. After running into Desmond at Bobel Cay and learning that he has their father aboard, Raib takes the old man, who has suffered a stroke, with him despite the extra burden this will impose on the *Eden.* Raib shows his soft side in his care for his father, an emissary of the old world, but he is harsh in dealing with his own men.

In fact, this harshness is the tragic flaw that leads to his own and their undoing. His constant tongue lashing drives Athens to jump ship, and his stubbornness lets Vemon suffer the consequences of his own behavior, losing two needed hands. His abuse of Brown culminates in his inability to keep his mouth shut when Brown was the only thing standing between the Jamaican pirates and his crew's safety, for Brown was in the process of subduing the Jamaicans with Captain Andrew's big knife when Raib called him a "Goddam thief" and demanded the knife. After the Jamaican leader then invites Brown to join them, "Got *pussy*, mahn! Got *rum!*" (*FT*, 345), Brown's allegiance hangs in the balance. Speedy tries to talk him into staying, but Brown remembers Raib's past insults, "Call me mon-fool! Call me *ladrón!*" And when Raib lashes out again, "Go den and good riddance!" (*FT*, 346), it is the breaking point. Brown slashes the throat of a green turtle in wanton anger and joins the Jamaicans. This resulting shift of power allows the Jamaicans to take control and ultimately forces the desperate night run through the Misteriosa Reefs.

If Raib is the voice of the novel in his lamentations over the changing of the times, Speedy is the corrective guide to Raib's tragic inflexibility and the indicator of how one must adapt to the modern world if one is to survive. As James Grove suggests, Speedy is "the only character who bridges the gap between old and modern times" (Grove, 25). Speedy frequently warns Raib that his abuse is going too far, and he shows Raib by example how one can hold the corruption of the modern at a distance from oneself without approving it or being driven to eradicate it. It was Speedy who came with Brown from Honduras. He has learned to coexist with disturbing change, and yet he is the most reliable, dependent and capable of the ship's crew—as Raib recognizes in praising him. Raib fails, however, to see another virtue in Speedy—tolerance, a virtue that would have made all the difference in Raib's keeping his men working for him and finally in keeping his tongue in check and his crew safe. Raib's rash bitterness toward Brown occasions the desperate situation that causes him to run the dangerous reefs under cover of darkness.

"De Bleak Ocean"   We must remember, before waxing philosophical, that the plight of the crew and captain of the *Eden* is a literal one. These are the dying days of the green-turtle industry, and the men are forced to go on long and precarious voyages in search of their catch. The *Eden*'s poor condition precisely mirrors the condition of the converted schooner on which Matthiessen went turtling: blind steering, no life preservers, no radio contact, no visible lights, ragged sails, and rotten rigging. As for the wind and the Jamaicans and the reefs, these are all part of the territory. So on a literal level, this story is about a vanishing and austere way of life, with affinities for other such ways of life that Matthiessen has reported on in a number of his works of nonfiction.

Of course, *Far Tortuga* does not stop on the literal level. The journey at sea, through threatening weather, past treacherous reefs, in search of the diminishing population of green turtles, creates a mythic atmosphere. The turtles themselves are beautiful and amazing creatures, ancient and gentle, better navigators than even the birds. And yet the hunting of the turtles by man seems part of a natural process that is unchallenged in the novel. The turtles begin life with the odds against survival, for only a small percentage make it back to the sea from their onshore hatching. Those who do must survive more predators in the shallow water before they are able to live and grow. As Bert Bender says, "the operant reality is clearly Darwinian. The image of life feeding on life surfaces everywhere throughout the novel . . ."[8] Sharks chase barracuda, which chase smaller fish, and so on. The green turtle, when it survives and grows into its magnificent size, still must face the perils of net and harpoon. In a sense, the turtle becomes an emblem of its human hunters aboard the *Eden.* Both are vanishing breeds, hemmed in by the dangers of nature.

More than once Raib refers to "de bleak ocean." In the reference is a sense of tragedy and inevitability. This is the ocean of *Riders to the Sea,* the ocean of *Moby-Dick,* the ocean of "The Open Boat." Specifically in its Caribbean setting, this is the ocean of boat-wrecking reefs and sudden storms. In order to survive in an ocean like this, a captain must know what he is doing. Raib is one of the best, as proud in his knowledge of the ocean as he is respectful of its powerful secrets. He is constantly reminding his crew of the ocean's mystery, using stories of days gone by to reinforce his message. And he himself attends carefully to the clues the ocean offers. One morning he puzzles about the signs he is receiving: "Dis mornin sea tryin to tell me something, Speedy. It so *old,* mon. Make me wonder what I doin way out here on dese reefs, all de days of my life. (*sighs*) Life has got away from me, some way—I just goin through de motions" (*FT,* 255). Raib's sigh is like the sigh of the green turtle, bound aboard the *Eden* and open-eyed, for Raib is just as bound to his ship and just as unenlightened in his fate. When Raib decides to go to the mysterious Far Tortuga, in the novel a legendary island whose ringed remnant of reefs is supposedly rife with turtles, he challenges the mysteries of nature. Yet only an excellent turtling spot can redeem the poor results thus far, and he is confident of his superior navigational ability. That he fails ultimately can be attributed to his hubris, his overreaching the normal boundaries. "Raib is also the victim of his greatness," says James Grove, comparing the Captain to Gatsby, Lord Jim, and Ahab: "In a sense, he attempts to become more than human, his greatness and tragedy rising out of his striving to capture the immortality he sees symbolized in the gulfweed" (Grove, 23). Captain Desmond, his nemesis, had warned him; and Wodie, his spiritual guide—although he refuses to admit it openly—also forecasts disaster. Raib is high on the mast when the ship hits the unexpected rock. He flies through the air and hits the deck just as had the flying fish that he had used as bait. His words to the fish while hooking them are emblematic of his own tragic flaw in the conflict between man and nature: "Fly too high, darlin, you fly too high" (*FT,* 91).

If Raib is a tragic figure in this conflict with "de bleak ocean," and I think he is, then Speedy once again is the salvific figure, illuminating the path of survival. Only Speedy lives through the shipwreck, because only Speedy was determined to survive and only Speedy acted with courage, decisiveness, and compassion. Determination is the most important ingredient, and Speedy refuses to believe at any point that he will do anything but survive. He knows where he is going, back to his land in Roatan, and he knows that somehow he will get there. He is fair to the other members of his catboat, but when Byrum tries to steal water, he kills him in a flash. He always said he was nicknamed Speedy for a reason. Afterward, he encourages Wodie to keep up his hope, but it is to no avail, for Wodie has already decided that his vision of the man in the blue boat signaled his end. At last, alone in the boat, Speedy sees the mainland. As a final gesture of respect for the nature that he has confronted and survived, Speedy cuts loose the green turtle and eases him into the water, countering the cruel slashing of the other turtle by his compatriot, Brown. Speedy becomes a foil for Brown's "modernity," as well as he has been a foil for Raib's proud bitterness. When he releases the turtle, he does so in a gesture of comradeship between lone survivors, both against the odds. Just as the lot of the turtles all along had paralleled that of the *Eden*'s crew, so it is at the end, for the remainder of the turtles went down with the ship. The ocean may be bleak, but there are qualities that contribute to survival. Speedy embodies those qualities of self-knowledge, determination, endurance, compassion, and decisiveness. The book ends with him safe on shore.

"Dat One Wild Rock"   The irony of the shipwreck of the *Eden* is that it occurs just after Captain Raib has successfully run past the treacherous Misteriosa Reefs. As the ship eases past the last of the shallow coral, Raib "flings his free arm wide, exalted. 'SHE CLEAR, SHE CLEAR! WE IN DE CLEAR!'" Just then, "The ship strikes" (*FT,* 367). While it is true that the ship need never have been in such dangerous straits were it not for Captain

Raib's tragic flaws and for Brown's betrayal, we must recognize that Raib did what he said he would do. He guided the ship safely through the reefs. It was a rock that was completely unknown, uncharted, and unpredictable that brought about the disaster. Raib, delirious after the accident, insists, "Ain't no rock dere. Ain't no coral in dat reach at all. We in de clear now, boys, we in de open water" (*FT,* 373). And Will Parchment confirms Raib's judgment, "He right, y'know," for Will had looked down into the water after the impact and seen only the darkness of deep water. Later Will tells Jim Eden, "your doddy done what he said he would do; he could not have known about dat one wild rock. We de first ones ever sailed out of Misteriosa Reefs in de night time and lived to tell de tale" (*FT,* 376). What Will has recognized is that some things at sea, and in life, are out of man's control. "Dat one wild rock" symbolizes the totally unexpected and uncontrollable calamities of life. It is a part of the natural world, "de bleak ocean," but it is a part not accessible to man's virtues of planning and control, for such rocks have not been charted. It is more mysterious even than the Misteriosa Reefs, for they at least could be navigated out of experience, old charts, and memory.

Matthiessen did not plot the disaster to occur in this way for the melodramatic effect of such a reversal. Rather the circumstances are meant to reflect the incalculable impact of chance on our lives. To conceive of the whole affair simply in terms of a tragedy brought on by human flaws would be untrue to Matthiessen's vision, which balances the roles of man's responsibilities and nature's whims in the outcome of human events. How else could we explain the safety of the drunken Vemon at Bragman's Point, or that of Athens and Brown? They will live to tell the tale of the *Eden,* along with Speedy, just as Will Parchment survived the *Majestic*'s sinking and told its tale to the *Eden*'s crew. Chance, of course, also played a role in Will's and Jim Eden's deaths, for they ended up in the leaky catboat, and a squall came up. Even Speedy, who did much to ensure his own survival, had the good fortune to flop into the sea-worthy boat after the rock was struck. He then survived all three of the perils that the crew and captain of the *Eden* had been faced with in *Far Tortuga*—the modern world, the natural world, and blind fate. Having adapted to "de modern time," struggled through "de bleak ocean," and escaped "dat one wild rock," Speedy is a figure of hope, Matthiessen's symbol of human potential. At the end he is a part of a picture of harmony of man and nature, "a figure alongshore, and white birds towarding" (*FT,* 408).

Chapter Eight

Zen Pilgrim: The Holy Places and the Stillness at the Center

The Snow Leopard, Nine-Headed Dragon River

The persistent paradox of Matthiessen's career is its combination of movement and stillness, action and contemplation, search and repose, fierce advocacy and monkish detachment, wildness and calm. Throughout his many
adventures and advocacies—the founding of the *Paris Review,* fishing commercially, trekking the jungles of South America and the wilds of Africa,
pursuing white shark and green turtle, espousing the causes of immigrant
workers and native Americans—there has been a waiting, a patience, a realization that what is important is not what is sought but the act of finding.
"All the way to heaven," Matthiessen likes to quote St. Catherine of Sienna
as saying, "is heaven." The line could be a gloss on Matthiessen's life and
one secret of its fullness, as well as an explanation of its antinomies, for
whether he is walking a picket line with Cesar Chavez, writing in his office,
or canoeing the Espiritu River, he lives every moment intensely. One senses
this in Matthiessen's attentive and direct gaze. It was even more noticeable
during my second visit to the Matthiessen household, when, in order to
make more time for our interview, I assisted him in raking sludge from "the
slough of despond," an old pond in his back yard that he is restoring. Suppressing my nervous instinct to break the silence, I gave myself to the dredg-
ing, content like my host to be one with the task.

Each individual has a unique and habitual way of orienting himself to the
outside world, which governs and colors each new experience. This attitude,
of course, is complex, with as many nuances and subtleties as there are in the
past experiences and beliefs that have shaped it. Matthiessen's basic orienta-
tion toward the world is one of watchfulness. It was in the eyes of the mature
man I met, and it was in the stare of the young boy whose living room windows "provided a grand view of the reservoirs and Central Park." In his essay
about growing up in New York, Matthiessen recalls: "In those days my perspective of New York revolved around Central Park, a seemingly infinite
expanse of greenery, lake and meadow stretching away from beneath our

windows to the shining battlements of the West Side" ("NY," 56). Note the words "infinite expanse" and "shining battlements" for their optimistic sense of possibilities. One can see, as well, in Matthiessen's childhood fascination with the greenery, lakes, and meadows of the park the vestigial impulse of his continual journeying to the world's wildernesses. In his boyish face, flush against the Fifth Avenue window, one discerns the lifelong attitude of quiet observation. From the beginning his eyes were unblinkingly open to the whole range of life's revelations, even unpleasant ones. He relates: "One day my brother and I were at the window when a woman stepped out between parked cars to cross Fifth Avenue. In a scene that is with me still, she was struck down with a terrible *bang* of flesh by a hurtling early morning taxi, which barely had time to screech its tires. Though whisked from the window by our nurse, we had witnessed death for the first time, and it was that vast metallic sound, as if the woman had attacked the taxi, that remains imprinted on my brain a half-century later" ("NY," 56). As he grew up, Matthiessen would continue his watchfulness, developing, from his boyhood summers on Fishers Island, a lifelong passion for observing birds.[1]

The watchful disposition shows itself everywhere in Matthiessen's writings, but it becomes more explicit after his embracing of Zen Buddhism in 1970. Zen gave his natural proclivity the support of a long and honorable religious tradition in its emphasis on enlightenment through the tangible and the particular. "The life of one day is a life to rejoice in," wrote the medieval Zen master Eihei Dogen, which Matthiessen quotes in the second of his two books that were directly influenced by his conversion to Zen. The corollary that the Zen master adds is: "If this one day in the lifetime of a hundred years is lost, will you ever get your hands on it again?" (*NHDR*, 60). Zen, in the writings of such masters and in the unbroken line of its teachers, provided Matthiessen with a religious context for his habitual posture toward the world.

In *The Snow Leopard* (1978) and *Nine-Headed Dragon River* (1985), Matthiessen confronts directly the terms of his spiritual search and his growing commitment to Zen Buddhism. His initial contact with Zen, during the late 1960s, was occasioned by the interest of his second wife, Deborah Love. Love and the writer had been going through nearly a decade of experimentation with hallucinogens and other drugs after the fashion of a spiritual odyssey, although Matthiessen admits they would never have called themselves "seekers": "We were embarrassed by such terms, and shied away from people who employed them" (*SL*, 45). About the same time the drug journey was wearing itself out, first for Love then for Matthiessen, the prospect of Zen loomed.

The transition from drugs to Zen had an internal logic, for the effects Matthiessen achieved by drugs prefigured, in a shadowy way, Zen's centering in the present. Matthiessen has always been careful in his explanations of his drug use, insisting that, while drugs may have harmed many and while he ultimately grew tired of what he calls their "magic carpet ride," the drug trip helped him clear away the burdens of the past. He comments on this explicitly in *The Snow Leopard,* stating that after each drug trip, "even the bad ones—I seemed to go more lightly on my way, leaving behind old residues of rage and pain" (*SL,* 47). When I asked Matthiessen about these residues in need of clearing, he explained that as a young man he had a lot of anger, that he constantly was getting into trouble at school, fighting, acting out. In his second year at Hotchkiss, he was "banished to a penitential corridor for chronic troublemakers" ("NY," 66). Drugs, in the 1960s, became for Matthiessen a kind of therapy, allowing him to go back into the past and put himself in touch with the buried sources of his rage. The ultimate effect of drugs then for Matthiessen was one of freedom; for, he avers, "drugs can clear away the past, enhance the present" (*SL,* 47). The author came to find, however, that the ride on drugs goes only so far "toward the inner garden" and that drugs bring their own obfuscation: "Old mists may be banished, that is true, but the alien chemical agent forms another mist, maintaining the separation of the 'I' from true experience of the One" (*SL,* 47).

The latter experience is at the core of Zen; and it is out of his ongoing commitment to Zen that Matthiessen wrote *The Snow Leopard* and *Nine-Headed Dragon River.* The former was based upon a 1973 trip to the Himalayas with biologist George Schaller, and it was published in 1978 after nearly eight years of Matthiessen's experience with Zen and six years of intense Zen meditation. The latter book, appearing in 1985, reflects nearly a decade of additional Zen practice, with over five years in the role of a Zen priest.

Personal testimony in matters of belief has a long history in the American literary tradition, going back to William Bradford's and John Winthrop's accounts of the early Puritan settlements. Jonathan Edwards's "Personal Narrative" is a landmark of spiritual history. And Ben Franklin's "Autobiography" serves the same purpose, although the focus of Franklin's writing is adjusted to the more worldly form of his soul. In the nineteenth century Thoreau's *Walden* stands out as a classic of the genre, for Thoreau's account is about how to live one's life, blending details of his physical experiment in the woods with testimony of his soul's satisfaction.

Despite their differences, *The Snow Leopard* and *Nine-Headed Dragon River* fall into this tradition of spiritual autobiography; in fact, the spiritual story is so integral to both that the "Buddhist" material in *The Snow Leopard* appears in *Nine-Headed Dragon River*. *The Snow Leopard,* in being based upon a particular adventure, is closer to *Walden,* the journey to Nepal and Tibet to visit the Crystal Monastery and perhaps glimpse the elusive snow leopard being Matthiessen's equivalent of Thoreau's experiment. *Nine-Headed Dragon River* is a less focused, less homogenous book, combining personal spiritual history with a larger historical picture of Zen. Whole sections read like Matthiessen's early *Wildlife in America* applied to Zen; but the final half of the book moves into the author's own journey to the holy places of Japan, blending historical interest with personal impressions. In both books, Matthiessen is the gentlest of witnesses, never a proselytizer, charting the course by which he has discovered the peacefulness of Zen against the background of excerpts from the Zen masters and the immediate experiences of the actual journey.

The Snow Leopard

Considered by many his best work, *The Snow Leopard* (1978) won the National Book Award in 1979. After *At Play in the Fields of the Lord,* it was also Matthiessen's most popular book, nesting for a time on the lower rungs of the best-seller lists. It might have been even more popular if the New York newspaper strike had not just started. Edward Hoagland's enthusiastic review occupied the front page of the *New York Times Book Review,* which never reached the stands.[2] Other reviewers as well were lavish with praise. Terrence Des Pres called the book "radiant" and "stunning" and waxed ecstatic over the "profound humanity of *The Snow Leopard,* a book fiercely felt and magnificently written, in which timelessness and 'modern time' are made to touch and join" (Des Pres, E4). And Jim Harrison said it was "a magnificent book: a kind of lunar paradigm and map of the sacred for any man's journey, where the snow leopard itself sits grail-like at the edge of consciousness, an infinitely stubborn koan in beast's clothing."[3]

If I had to recommend one book of Matthiessen's to the uninitiated, it would be *The Snow Leopard,* for it is more personal and more integrative of Matthiessen's whole life and thought than any of his other writings. The book gathers together all the major concerns and interests of his other nonfiction in their most profound formulation and most compelling symbolic expression. Everything is there: a journey to a remote area of the world, close observation of the wild landscapes, an appreciation of and tribute to the indigenous peoples and their cultures, reflections both topical and universal, and an overriding metaphor that emerges from the trip. In addition, *The*

Snow Leopard couches all of this in a voice at once more intensely intimate and more clearly evocative of spiritual forebears than that of the other books.

Matthiessen's journey this time is to the Crystal Mountain in northwestern Nepal. Invited by biologist George Schaller, who was interested in studying the rare bharal, or Himalayan blue sheep, which are said to be plentiful in the area, Matthiessen internalizes the trip as a "true pilgrimage, a journey of the heart" (*SL*, 3); at Crystal Mountain is the Crystal Monastery and a revered Buddhist holy man, the Lama of Shey. Both Schaller and Matthiessen have added incentive for the trip in their hopes of catching a glimpse of "that rarest and most beautiful of the great cats, the snow leopard" (*SL*, 3), which preys upon the blue sheep. The trip occurred in 1973, and Matthiessen uses the most direct form of narration, a daily journal, starting 28 September and ending 1 December.

On the simplest level, Matthiessen's account is a travelogue of his and Schaller's two hundred and fifty-mile walk across the pale grey and brown Himalayan high country. Their progress and their encounters provide the bulk of the narrative, and on this level it resembles Schaller's own account, the final chapter of his *Stones of Silence*.[4] As usual Matthiessen's eye is sharp, and his interaction with his surroundings intense. With him we come upon a community in the deep inner canyons of the Himalaya, whose dwellings are all contained in one stepped pueblo on a hillside, with the roofs of one family the terrace of another, "the levels connected by crude ladders hewn in a single log" (*SL*, 81). Strangely, the inhabitants completely ignore the travelers, "pretending we are not there" (*SL*, 82). Such enigmas, we are led to believe, are small manifestations of the wider mystery of the sacred mountains and the people who live in their shadow.

Schaller and Matthiessen discover an unexpected pack of wolves frisking and playing on the mountain slopes: "two silver wolves, and two of faded gold, and one that is the no-color of frost: this frost-colored wolf, a big male, seems to be leader. All have black tail tips and a delicate black fretting on the back" (*SL*, 195). Both men are delighted by the appearance of the wolves, an Asian variety of the Alaska timber wolf, "always an exciting animal." Matthiessen himself seems surprised to learn from Schaller that the wolves will hunt and kill not only blue sheep, but fox and leopard as well. The next day, through their binoculars, the pair watch two wolves hunt and attack a herd of blue sheep, isolating one prospective victim, and "flying down across the cliffs" in attack before the sheep "scoots free and gains a narrow ledge where no wolf can follow" (*SL*, 198). Matthiessen is elegant in his descriptions of such occurrences and their aftermath: "In the frozen air, the whole mountain is taut; the silence rings. The sheep's flanks quake, and the wolves are panting; otherwise, all is still, as if the arrangement of pale shapes held the world together. Then I breathe, and the mountain breathes, setting the world in motion once again" (*SL*, 198).

One of the author's greatest gifts is his ability both to experience nature fully and to tell about it in the choicest language. He has always had this ability, from his earliest books on American wildlife, but here in *The Snow Leopard* he is at the height of his sympathetic union with his surroundings and of his finding the equivalent for this experience in the sounds and rhythms of his sentences. Apparently Zen meditation intensified Matthiessen's already intense participation in the natural world. Whatever the explanation, he has never been more fully Emerson's Poet, who "sees and handles that which others dream of" with the power "to receive and to impart" ("The Poet," 219).

Although the book is at least as rich as his other travel books in such observation, description, and information, it also reaches deeper into the author's soul than any of the others. The death of his wife, Deborah, in 1972 set the emotional stage of this journey to the sacred mountains of the east, as the death of Thoreau's beloved brother, John, had preceded his withdrawal to Walden. The impact of her dying had been complicated by the turmoil of their relationship, breaking a longtime emotional logjam in Matthiessen. The release continues during the course of his Himalayan walk, which becomes a journey through grief and back to healthy living. At one point, as he sits against the mountain-side resting in the sun, tears spontaneously flow. He reflects, "All this *feeling* is astonishing: not so long ago I could say truthfully that I had not shed a tear in twenty years" (*SL*, 115).

Matthiessen's walk is, in a sense, a retreat from life, allowing recovery and renewal. Again echoing the call of Thoreau to "simplify, simplify, simplify," Matthiessen says, "I long to let go, drift free of things, to accumulate less, depend on less, to move more simply" (*SL*, 126). He has cut himself off from the outside world to such an extent that he loses track of the day of the week, and "the great events that must be taking place in the world we left behind are as illusory as events from a future century. It is not so much that we are going back in time as that time seems circular, and past and future have lost meaning" (*SL*, 126). Having experienced one loss, Matthiessen senses the universality of loss. Time, possessions, even human attachments are all subject to eventual passing, so they must be viewed in the light of eternity. Thoughts of death, which haunt Matthiessen during his journey, intensify and come to a point when he is faced with a narrow ledge in an exhausted state. He wavers between timidity and boldness, reminding himself of his own responsibilities, "for I have young children with no mother, and much work to finish; but these aren't honest reasons, past a point. Between clinging and letting go, I feel a terrific struggle. This is a fine chance to let go, to 'win my life by losing it,' which means not recklessness but acceptance, not passivity but nonattachment" (*SL*, 147–48). The key here is his recognition that crossing the ledge is not recklessness, but acceptance, and that to turn back would be a craven clinging, not responsible action. After proceeding down the ridge, Matthiessen watches a lizard on a streamside rock, realizing that the rock was once under the sea, and that the flood of water is wearing it away "to return it once again into the oceans" (*SL*, 148). We are indeed impelled by larger forces, and the only sensible path is that of acceptance.

Through these and like reflections Matthiessen resolves his grief, faces his own mortality, and moves on. The theme of movement, continuing in the course of the journey, is an important one. Eventually he says good-bye not only to his wife who died, but also to his first wife: "In the autumnal melancholy I remember France, in the years that I lived there, still in love with my first wife. One day in Paris, I met Deborah Love, whom I was to marry ten years later. And now, in different ways, those life-filled creatures are both gone. I hurry with the river" (*SL*, 291–92).

The book is indeed a kind of spiritual autobiography, at once a reflection on the significant spiritual experiences of his life and at the same time an ultimate enactment of the spiritual dynamic that has informed most of that life. The autobiographical reflection comes in spurts, the most prominent of which occurs for the entry of 5 October. After the usual comment on the day's progress and their surroundings, Matthiessen notes how divided is his present mental state, one self observing, one self remembering his son Alex, one self trying to sleep. The thought of Alex recalls a particular memory of him standing rapt in his sandbox and expands into a reflection on how easily and naturally the child becomes one with things around him, "unaware of endings and beginnings, still in unison with the primordial nature of creation, letting all light and phenomena pour through. Ecstasy is identity with all existence . . ." (*SL*, 41). Obviously shaped by his Zen apprenticeship, but also by his own journey through life, Matthiessen defines this union with creation as the archetypal religious experience, expanding on it in a marvelous passage that echoes his American predecessors, Emerson and Thoreau, as well as his Zen masters: "Amazingly, we take for granted that instinct for survival, fear of death, must separate us from the happiness of pure and uninterpreted experience, in which body, mind, and nature are the same. And this debasement of our vision, the retreat from wonder, the backing away like lobsters from free-swimming life into safe crannies, the desperate instinct that our life passes unlived, is reflected in proliferation without joy, corrosive money rot, the gross befouling of the earth and air and water from which we came" (*SL,* 42).

From there Matthiessen goes on to chronicle his seminal glimpse of this experience on board a U.S. navy ship in the Pacific (quoted at length in chapter 1) and his subsequent search for understanding in the works of Hamsun, Borges, Thoreau, Hesse, and Kierkegaard. His was Kierkegaard's "'sickness of infinitude,' wandering from one path to another with no real recognition that I was embarked upon a search, and scarcely a clue as to what I might be after" (*SL,* 43). In 1948, Matthiessen was introduced to the work of the mystic-philosopher George Gurdjieff, which emphasized "paying attention to the present moment instead of wandering the ephemeral worlds of past and future"; but Gurdjieff's work was too esoteric, and Matthiessen admits "my confused state is plain in my first books" (*SL,* 43). In 1959 began nearly a decade of regular drug use, journeys clearly motivated by the search for significance in the present moment, but passages now seen by Matthiessen as only illusory of real religious experience. The return to "home," to the commonplace self, the inner law, came to Matthiessen as the key through reading a passage from Jung, which said that a man must obey his own law "as if it were a daemon whispering to him of new and wonderful paths. . . . The only meaningful life is a life that strives for the individual realization—absolute and unconditional—of its own particular law. . . . To the extent that a man is untrue to the law of his being . . . he has failed to realize his life's meaning."[5] Matthiessen says he was so excited by this passage that "I actually yelled and jumped out of my chair: this searching was not morbid after all!" (*SL,* 45).

It is obvious from the commentary of *The Snow Leopard* that his searching has led him to Zen, which has become *the* way for Matthiessen, who is now a Zen priest. The book is dedicated to three Zen teachers, and the journey it describes is a pilgrimage to the Crystal Monastery and the Lama of Shey. That Matthiessen does not at first recognize the latter because of his commonplace appearance ("the *tulku,* or incarnate Lama, whom I was so anxious to find, is none other than the crippled monk who was curing the goat skin in yak butter and brains" [*SL,* 229]) contains an important Zen lesson, and one which has been present throughout Matthiessen's other writings as well. The significant things are frequently encountered in ordinary and unexpected places, usually while we are pursuing something with a grander, more exalted countenance. Shortly after meeting the Lama a second time, now in his proper circumstances, Matthiessen reflects on the "common miracles—the murmur of my friends at evening, the clay fires of smudgy juniper, the coarse dull food, the hardship and simplicity, the contentment of doing one thing at a time: when I take my blue tin cup into my hand, that is all I do" (*SL*, 232). The discovery of these common miracles has been made possible by the lack of distraction from the outside world, allowing focus on the present. Matthiessen realizes that "gradually my mind has cleared itself, and wind and sun pour through my head, as through a bell. Though we talk little here, I am never lonely; I am returned into myself" (*SL*, 232). The whole experience sounds like an Ignatian long retreat I once underwent, that month-long withdrawal from society and conversation to contemplate one's life against the background of ultimate things. Also reminiscent of Ignatius of Loyola and the whole Christian mystic tradition is Matthiessen's emphasis on the emptying of self, a bridge between the spirituality of east and west.

Matthiessen never glimpses the snow leopard, and the animal therefore becomes symbolic both of nature at its wildest (and least accessible) and the ultimate beatific vision (*kensho*), for which Matthiessen admits he was not ready. "I am disappointed, and also I am not disappointed. That the snow leopard *is,* that it is here, that its frosty eyes watch us from the mountain—that is enough" (*SL*, 242). This is a remarkable statement from a man who has made a good part of his living from observing wild creatures and reporting about it.

Ironically, the book named after a creature that is neither photographed nor seen would become one of his most popular works. It is the ultimate evolution of a change that began when Matthiessen decided to leave his camera home when he traveled (beginning with *The Tree Where Man Was Born,* his photographs no longer appear). Asked about the decision, he said, "The camera is a different way of seeing." Clearly the writing way is less acquisitive, less proprietary. Had the great white shark not shown himself in *Blue Meridian,* there would have been little complacence. Yet, now, the snow leopard's remaining unseen becomes a victory of nature, retaining some power over man's probing eyes, that Matthiessen can be satisfied with.

His complacence over not seeing the snow leopard also exemplifies the Zen acceptance of *what is,* which is so graphically demonstrated by the Lama of Shey. The Lama, when asked if he is happy here in the remote isolation of Tsakang, unable to leave because of the severe arthritic condition of his legs, answers: "Of course I am happy here! It's wonderful! *Especially* when I have no choice!" (*SL*, 246). Toward the end of the journey Matthiessen has another realization that enforces the same message of acceptance, as well as repeating the dynamic of the unexpected miracle that had always been there if we only had eyes. It is that Tukten, faithful Sherpa—not the Lama of Shey—has been Matthiessen's true teacher throughout this whole adventure. Tukten is he who Buddhists say "will appear." Matthiessen eventually comes to understand that "in his life in the moment, in his freedom from attachments, in the simplicity of his everyday example, Tukten has taught me over and over, he is the teacher that I hoped to find . . ." (*SL*, 316). If he had been ready, Matthiessen thinks, Tukten might have led him even to the vision of the snow leopard.

Here, as in his other nonfiction, Matthiessen's greatest affinity is with his native guide. With his biologist companion on the trip, George Schaller, Matthiessen retains a cordial, if distant, relationship. Matthiessen says, "We have been on different journeys, and mostly we have worked alone, which suits us both, and even in the evenings, we talked little" (*SL*, 265). Matthiessen's journey was personal and religious, finding in the everyday example of the simple Sherpa Tukten a living wisdom that embodied the Zen teachings he had been assimilating over the past three years. Tukten, like the Indians of North and South America, the Inuit of Nunivak Island, the Kurelu of New Guinea, lives out of a wisdom deriving from his closeness to the earth. The real insight he brings, however, is that one need not search in faraway places or in extraordinary events for enlightenment. The path of true knowledge runs through the ordinary. In the dwindling days of his Himalayan venture, Matthiessen suspects "this is what Tukten knows—that the journey to Dolpo, step by step and day by day, is the Jewel in the Heart of the Lotus, the Tao, the Way, the Path, but no more so than small events of days at home" (*SL*, 300). The realization allows Matthiessen a new freedom in his own life and in his travels hereafter, a freedom from the compulsive need to get to the bottom of things, to plunge into the deepest parts of the ocean, or the furthest outbacks of the wilderness. When and if nature is ready, like the snow leopard, it will reveal its secrets. Meanwhile, we have only, like Tukten Sherpa, to shoulder our daily portage and keep watchful. Perhaps we shall see, as does Matthiessen and two sherpas, something rare like the red panda, "the loveliest of all forest animals in the Himalaya" (*SL*, 306), this unexpected vision a reward at the end of their journey. If so, we should rejoice. If not, we should accept "the failures of this journey as well as . . . its wonders . . ." (*SL*, 301).

Nine-Headed Dragon River: Zen Journals 1969–1982

As the subtitle informs, this book tracks the author's own footprints through the fields of Zen, "the religion before religion" (*NHDR*, ix). However, it is also a compendium of information about the formation and development of Zen theory and practice, particularly about Zen's transplanting here in the United States. Because the book serves two purposes, one personal, the other historical, it is less unified and less effective than most of Matthiessen's works. Its publication by Shambhala Press rather than by a commercial publisher suggests that *Nine-Headed Dragon River* issues from a personal debt that Matthiessen felt to his spiritual teachers and from a desire to fill a gap in our knowledge of the master-pupil heritage of Zen transmission. The book does not have the pull and adventure readers of Matthiessen have come to expect, for it is framed by a spiritual rather than a physical journey. The last section does, however, trace Matthiessen and his teacher Tetsugen's trip to the major monasteries of Japan, climaxing with their reception by Matthiessen's old teacher, now returned to deep seclusion, the eccentric and electric Soen-roshi ("roshi" means senior teacher, and "sensei" means teacher, and in Zen practice the title is affixed to the teacher's name as a sign of respect).

One cannot read the book and not absorb considerable knowledge of Zen. As Matthiessen and Tetsugen travel across Japan, its ancient Buddhist shrines become occasions of information about Buddhism's inception in that country in the 600s in a non-Zen form, and later its evolution into the two main sects of Zen, Soto and Rinzai. We meet not only the present-day masters, limned against their ancient monasteries and landscapes, but also, through anecdote and quotation, the great historical figures in the tradition, especially Dogen Zenji, the thirteenth-century Soto Zen master. In fact, it is the ancient places associated with Dogen Zenji that are the destinations of Matthiessen's pilgrimage. Although his works had been largely neglected until recently, Dogen has come to be regarded as the most powerful thinker in the Zen tradition, and, according to Matthiessen, one of the "most exciting minds in the history of thought" (*NHDR*, 137). We are told that one of Dogen's most important teachings is the immanence of enlightenment in even the most ordinary acts of daily life ("Buddha-nature is not some kind of changeless entity, but is none other than the eternally rising and perishing reality of the world" [*NHDR*, 167]). Dogen is insisting on "the wonderful precision of this present moment, moment after moment—*now*" (*NHDR*, 167). The text is richly strewn with citations from Dogen Zenji, so much so that it seems obvious that part of Matthiessen's intention was to make Dogen's thought more widely available. My own favorite quote concretely illustrates his previous statement about Buddha-nature: "Each and every extraordinary activity is simply having rice. . . . Inheriting the buddhas' essential wisdom is realizing the activity of having rice" (*NHDR*, 247).

In his account of Zen history in America, Matthiessen credits Emerson and Thoreau for making the ground fertile for the later growth of Zen communities. He says that the American transcendentalists "led the way in a wider study of what Emerson called 'the wise silence, the universal beauty, to which every part and particle is equally related, the eternal One.' Emerson confessed to a 'sky-void idealism,' in apparent reference to the Mahayana concept of universal 'emptiness,' the Oneness that includes everything; this sky-void he equated with 'the Eternal Buddha'" (*NHDR*, 10). And Thoreau was equally inspired, Matthiessen says, by "my Buddha," wishing "to go soon and live away by the pond, where I shall hear only the wind whispering among the reeds. It will be a success if I shall have left my self behind" (*NHDR*, 10–11). To see the names of Emerson and Thoreau cropping up in yet another Matthiessen book reinforces their influence on him and the firm placement of his work within their tradition. Their emphasis on simplicity, immediacy, and loss of self in the One are the Zen side of a legacy that includes such other influencing ideas as the healing power of nature, the importance of self-reliance, and the writer's duty to build his own world out of his experience.

On the personal level, *Nine-Headed Dragon River* works as a kind of religious testimony. Matthiessen is clearly out to give an account of his own Zen practice, which has "delighted me and refreshed my life" in order that "others may be drawn toward the path of Zen" (*NHDR*, ix). Since part of his spiritual evolution was recounted in *The Snow Leopard*, those sections reappear as chapters 7 and 8, although the story of Matthiessen's initial attraction to Zen through his second wife is told here in greater detail, as well as the account of her subsequent illness and death, a dying made more bearable by their mutual Zen commitment.

The early period of Matthiessen's Zen practice involved intense meditation in the strict Rinzai sect. After six such years, he ceased attending *sesshins* for two years, instead polishing his Himalayan journals into the form of *The Snow Leopard*, which he said took the place of meditation. Part of what was happening during this period, Matthiessen later realized, was disaffection with his Rinzai teacher, eventuating in his turning to the Soto sect. The latter, placing more emphasis on just "sitting meditation" rather than the use of koan study with its challenging riddles, is less rigorous and exact than the Rinzai sect, with its shouting and use of the warning stick to enforce its discipline. In early 1977, Matthiessen manifested his formal interest in Soto by attending a *sesshin* at the Zen Center of Los Angeles. At about this same time, Matthiessen made another significant change in his Zen habits, ceasing to record with meticulous accuracy the spiritual ebbs and flows of his meditation practice "with their hoarding of miraculous states and 'spiritual attainments,' with their contaminating clinging, their insidious fortification of the ego" (*NHDR*, 130). In June of 1979, the seeds of a Soto Zen community in the New York region were sown by a *sesshin* conducted by Tetsugen-sensei with Matthiessen's assistance. It was at this time that Tetsugen became Matthiessen's teacher. In 1981, Matthiessen's head was shaved in ordination to the Zen priesthood.

The style of the book is as clean and sharp as most of Matthiessen's writings, but it is not as easy to follow because it lacks a narrative pull. Also, the alternation between spiritual journey and Zen history creates a disjunction. The book's movement, however, is intentionally slow and ruminative—to be read in snatches, perhaps even contemplatively, for the thoughts are generative and worth the time. Each chapter begins with quotations from Dogen Zenji, confirming the high regard of his Zen devotees. The marvelous thing about Zen, something that comes across in the book and something that Matthiessen spoke about to an audience in Watertown, Massachusetts, in February 1989, is its accessibility to people from all different beliefs. It is less a religion than an awareness, a state of mind. Dogen writes: "There is an extremely easy way to become Buddha. Refraining from all evil, not clinging to birth or death, working in deep compassion for all sentient beings, respecting those over you and pitying those below you, without any detesting or desiring, worrying or lamentation—this is what is called Buddha. Do not search beyond it" (*NHDR*, 30).

The book is beautifully produced with a helpful glossary of Zen terminology, an index, and a map of the author's trip across Japan. In all, this is a book to keep, refer to for facts about Zen's history and Matthiessen's spiritual evolution, and return to for nuggets of Zen wisdom.

Chapter Nine
The Return to Fiction

On the River Styx and Other Stories,
Killing Mister Watson

With the appearance of a collection of stories in 1989 and a novel in 1990, Matthiessen has returned to his first and highest calling, fiction. His first publication was a story, "Sadie" (*Atlantic,* January 1951), and his first book a novel, *Race Rock* (1952). Yet the preponderance of his writing in the intervening years has been nonfiction, for he published only two novels in the 1960s, one in the 1970s, and none in the 1980s. Most of the stories in *On the River Styx and Other Stories* (1989) appeared in print more than twenty-five years ago; two of them, however, the title story and "Lumumba Lives," were written recently, marking the definitive turn in Matthiessen's many alternations between fiction and nonfiction. In the preface to *Styx,* the author admits that in the last two decades he has written "a bit too much nonfiction,"[1] echoing a remark he made to me in August 1989, that his major concentration henceforth would be fiction. The first product of that concentration is *Killing Mister Watson,* a novel comparable in original-ity and scale to his major achievements in the genre.

On the River Styx and Other Stories

Matthiessen's is a polished and varied collection, spanning nearly forty years of short-story writing. Although he has written three times their num-ber, the ten stories comprising the book represent the only ones now satisfac-tory to their author. As a whole, the collection exhibits a wide range of subject matter and characterization, an unflinching realism, and consum-mate artistry in language. Matthiessen writes about a man wanting to buy a hunting dog, two men searching for a drowned body, a fourteen-year-old boy's Christmas, a marriage coming apart, a manhunt, a wolf hunter's last hunt, the complementary antagonism of two men at sea, a volunteer work-er's attachment to a patient who does not belong in a mental hospital, an eastern couple's fishing trip to Florida, and a foreign service operative's return to the estate his family once owned. Each story is built around a confrontation that both reveals and transforms character. "The Fifth Day" features two men arguing over whether they should expend energy rowing their skiff in search of a drowned man or simply wait for the corpse to surface, as the more experienced says bodies always do, on the fifth day. Once this conflict is resolved by the emergence of the body as predicted, the tension shifts to the contrast between the searchers' inward indifference and their outward respect for the dead man and his family. In "The Centerpiece," set in 1941, a teenage boy watches his cousin refuse to take part in their grandmother's Germanic celebration of Christmas. The girl's protest, motivated by wartime patriotism, is made light of by the grandmother ("The child is far too young to take a stand on *anything*" [*ORS,* 27]), but in the end youthful idealism triumphs, for the older woman no longer insists on calling it a German Christmas.

The early stories are good, but they are small, and one advantage of the collection's chronological arrangement is that we can chart Matthiessen's growth as a writer of short fiction. He says in the Preface, "one hopes that in close to forty years there has been a little bit of progress" (*ORS,* x). Indeed, there has. And, while this progress has not been as dramatic as the leap from the early novels to the later ones, it is of the same order. As in the early novels, Matthiessen's style in his early stories was always intact, proving him a master of dialogue and dialect with that first story, "Sadie." In using the first-person voice of good old boy Les Webster about his attempt to buy some hunting dogs, the Yale creative writing student demonstrated his control of other voices and his ability to be objective: "I didn't feel much like looking at Dewey Floyd right then, so I looked at the ground. All I could see was the stick switching back and forth, back and forth, in the dust in front of his shoes. It made me jumpier'n hell, and I glanced up at him. I saw his face. And I'm tellin you right now, it ain't that nigger boy beat Pentland to death, I don't care *what* they say" (*ORS,* 12–13). Matthiessen's restraint in the early stories is surprising for a young writer, although there is an occasional lapse into verbal acrobatics, as when the boy narrator of "The Centerpiece" says: "I had winnowed my presents from a heap which cornucopiaed from the base of the spruce to the shoulder of the hearth, and was engaged in arraying them in good order for opening" (*ORS,* 26).

The stories clearly fall into three periods. The early group (four stories), written between 1950 and 1953, deal with carefully couched conflicts that remain subdued and controlled. Their manifestations are interior, and the tone of these stories is cool. For example, in "Late in the Season," we feel the palpable tension between Cici and Frank Avery, but its only external sign is a dead turtle and a little boy crying. And "The Fifth Day"'s effectiveness derives from all of the scorn that is suppressed in Joe Robitelli's respectful removal of his cap. In the second group of four stories (1957–63), conflict bubbles over into violence. In "Travelin Man"—a story reminiscent of, but more realistic than, Richard Connell's suspenseful "The Most Dangerous Game"—an escaped black prisoner is tracked and killed by a white hunter. In "The Wolves of Aguila," a surrealist mood story, violence returns to the wolf hunter as nature mysteriously vindicates herself. "Horse Latitudes" shows two men held together by a dislike that manifests itself in increasing verbal violence. And "Midnight Turning Grey" displays the volcanic frustration of a sane man cast into a mental institution, his internal pressure finally erupting and making him one with his environment.

In his first stage of short fiction, Matthiessen is an artist and a delineator of conflicts just below the surface. In his second stage, he is equally artistic, but his emotional range enlarges as the conflict becomes more external. It is in the third stage, however, his two most recent stories, "On the River Styx" and "Lumumba Lives," that Matthiessen fully melds language and emotional range into themes of greater significance. Racial disharmony is the focus of the stories; and although Matthiessen had touched on this theme in his earlier "Sadie" and "Travelin Man," it was not with the later breadth of vision.

"On the River Styx" is a long story about an environmental lawyer, Burkett, and his wife, Alice, as they go to the Ten Thousand Islands area in South Florida to do a little snook fishing. The story revolves around racial tension between this liberal easterner, his black guide, Dickie, and the white town leaders, especially Judge Jim Whidden, who has things his way in the community, where black folks supposedly like to keep to themselves and know their place even if liberal eastern lawyers don't. The tension starts when Burkett tries to befriend Dickie, who acts surly and distant until, on their second outing, Burkett shares rum with him. Dickie, considerably loosened, turns from distant to overfamiliar, helping himself to food from their hamper; and when the couple return to their cabin for the night, they notice that the remaining rum and Alice's tape recorder are missing. While they resent the distinct moods of Dickie (sullen to them, obsequious to Whidden, imperious to other blacks) and can't help but think he took both things (especially when out fishing the next day he miraculously produces the rum bottle, with little left), they also don't want to get him into any trouble because they detect such strong racism in the white townsmen. Whidden, for example, flaunts the word "nigger" until out of mock sensitivity he changes it to "nigra"; and when coffee is served, the locals ask if one wants it black or integrated. When Burkett directly questions Dickie about the tape deck, his response is denial, "Nawsuh, nawsuh, ain't seen nothin, nawsuh!" (*ORS,* 156). Once the Judge finds out about the missing tape player, he vows to get to the bottom of it over Burkett's protests; after all, he says, "how can I show folks a dandy time when their personal propitty ain't safe, even?" (*ORS,* 159). When Whidden collars another black, Johnny, for the theft, Burkett goes straight to Dickie and accusingly demands he return the tape deck directly to him before both he and Johnny, who apparently had been handed the recorder and was returning it when he was caught by Whidden, get into bad trouble. It is at this point in the story, in his exasperation with Dickie, that Burkett wants to yell at him "Stupid damn nigger!" (*ORS,* 166). When he returns home, however, a paper bag has been taken from under their cabin by Dickie and placed on the steps. In it is the tape recorder, allowing Burkett to go to Whidden pretending he had merely misplaced it and apologizing for all the trouble. Whidden, of course, realizes the ploy: "You ain't so smart as you think you are. . . . This business ain't finished by a long shot" (*ORS,* 167). Burkett leaves, and Dickie is summoned into Whidden's office at the story's end: "You, goddamnit, Dickie, get on in here!" (*ORS,* 167).

The story captures the not so subtle racial strains in a southern rural town and the eastern liberal's inability to relate to the blacks or remedy the inequities. At the same time, the lawyer comes to a realization of his own vestigial racism in his anger at the guide's stupidity. The story is totally realistic in its setting among the mangrove swamps that lead out toward the Gulf of Mexico, the same setting used in *Killing Mister Watson*: "this small fishing settlement at the far end of an eight-mile canal road was the 'last frontier town' at the edge of 'the last wilderness' of the Ten Thousand Islands" (*ORS,* 140). Dialogue and description bring the place and its inhabitants alive in inflection and appearance. It is a wonderfully effective story, especially in Matthiessen's accurate portrait of the high-principled environmental lawyer and his critical wife, and in its unerring portrait of racial dynamics. The title's allusion to the River Styx is derived from Alice Burkett's comment that they are being poled through the dark islets by "their silent boatman." It takes a larger meaning, however, in that the racial strife of the story is hinted to be the dark underworld of modern life.

"Lumumba Lives," 1990's second prize O. Henry Award story, is a luminous tale about recovering the past, man's abuse of nature, and the chasm of color that divides America. If that seems like a lot, it is; however, this is a large story in length (nearly forty pages) as well as breadth, and the three thematic strains are blended harmoniously. Unquestionably this is Matthiessen's finest short story and is destined, I believe, to become a modern classic.

Like an overture, the opening lines hit the major chords with their ominous simplicity: "He comes by train out of the wilderness of cities, he has come from abroad this very day. At mid-life he has returned to a hometown where he knows no one" (*ORS*, 168). Henry Harkness returns home to what once was the family estate on the upper Hudson, buying the old gardener's house to refurbish and live in. He has been in the foreign service in Africa, having worked covertly to topple Lumumba and install a pro-American ruler in his stead, causing a break with his father, formerly the Assistant Secretary for African Affairs and from an older and more principled school of foreign policy. Now Henry has been relieved of his African assignment, apparently out of favor in the service despite his faithful dirty work. Coming from professional failure abroad, he returns to discover American society's failure to achieve rapport between blacks and whites. Racial tension is thicker than the air's and the river's pollution, which has also increased. "Looking north, he thinks, The river has lost color" (*ORS*, 168). Color, however, is in the forefront of the white residents' thinking. When he tells the clerk that he is from Africa, the response is: "You'll feel right at home, then . . . Goddam Afros overflowing right out of the city. Come up this way from Yonkers, come up at night along the river" (*ORS*, 169). Later racial prejudice becomes more palpable in the jokes he hears from the white real-estate agent and others.

Harkness is out of place, having lost his continuity with his privileged past, uneasy with the white residents that surround him, out of kilter with his natural surroundings, and disillusioned by the course of his career. As he looks "across the water to the cliffs where Rip Van Winkle had slept for twenty years," he becomes a figure of Rip himself, awakening to the real world of America after having been gone for so long. "He peers across the mile of water, as if that shelter high up in clean mountains were still there" (*ORS*, 181). In order to recapture something of the purity of the magical and legendary past, Harkness decides to have a final and ritual duck supper, in memory of the hunts of his youth with his father. After this, he will never hunt again, so he buys the minimal equipment and goes out one morning to shoot a duck, which he does, but the duck falls into the river, and he cannot retrieve it. The thought of it being wasted, of his not using that which was killed (again from his father), impels him into a foolish, nearly self-destructive plunge into the Hudson while some nearby black fishermen look on. They are ostensibly friendly, but he is convinced they want his hidden wallet and gun. One of them wears a T-shirt with "Lumumba Lives" across its front. Harkness, who realizes that he never liked Lumumba personally, reacts with hostile abandon, even taunting the men about the shirt, "Wholumumba, wholumumba, wholumumba, WHO!" (ORS, 202). They follow him until he pulls the gun on them in threat. Sensing his craziness, they back off, except for the youngest, Frag, who tracks him back to the house with Henry suddenly aware of him, then seeking a bloody confrontation, perhaps the fulfillment of his earlier suggestion to the agent that one dead nigger burglar would do a lot more for the neighborhood safety than all those security alarms and lights. Henry Harkness finds himself backed into a corner, out of communion with his family's past and the pure vision of America's early years when Henry Hudson's river was blue and "swirled with silver fishes" and when Rip Van Winkle's "shelter high up in clean mountains [was] still there" (ORS, 180, 1).

The story's last sentence expresses starkly the increasingly embattled situation of the American white landowner: "Still he waits there in the autumn garden, cooling his forehead on the night-blue metal, in the haunted sunlight, in the dread of home" (ORS, 208). It is a magnificent line. Henry, knowing that Frag is out there in the night and that at some moment he will come, waits with his gun at hand. The Harkness estate, which is located in the town of Arcadia, represents the Puritan vision of paradise achieved through hard work and virtue. Significantly, it is now abandoned, broken up into private fortresses called homes. The Garden of Eden, the settler's vision of America, is in the decline of autumn, and the sunlight is haunted by dark specters of racial enemies as well as dark specters of the mind. Home is a dread place because it offers no real security despite the momentary comfort of weaponry.

After reading part of "Lumumba Lives" at the Interface Center in Watertown, Massachusetts, in January 1988, Matthiessen commented that the problem facing America today is that of race. In the final two stories of his collection, he has imaginatively assessed this problem in both southern and northern settings. It is not an optimistic picture. He has drawn images of liberal white America confounded by the actualities of racial tension and turning away in either consternation ("On the River Styx") or retrenchment ("Lumumba Lives").

Killing Mister Watson

Killing Mister Watson (1990), Matthiessen's return to long fiction after a fifteen-year hiatus, is his third major novel. With At Play in the Fields of the Lord (1965) and Far Tortuga (1975), it balances nicely the trio of earlier and decidedly minor novels written while Matthiessen was in his twenties. Twenty-five years separate the first and last of the major novels, none published within ten years of another. Matthiessen might churn out his nonfiction, but he proceeds with utmost deliberation in his novel writing. *Far Tortuga* was an achievement of such technical virtuosity and symbolic resonance that one can understand the author's reluctance to plunge into another novel soon thereafter. The latest book, however, draws on new energies; and, while it may not be as experimental as *Far Tortuga,* it is daring enough technically, employing a narration of multiple first-person reminiscences that are bound together by the third-person account of a fictitious historian. *Killing Mister Watson* also is Matthiessen's only major novel with an American setting, giving a national, societal dimension to some of his abiding concerns.

The story is based upon the life and death of Edgar J. Watson, a historical figure of legendary mystery and power, who was killed by the members of his rural, coastal Florida community in 1910. This central act of violence, which is revealed at the outset in the book's only objectively narrated section, controls the entire story by its enigma. On one level, the novel is a mystery, not a whodunit, for we know who the killers are right from the start, but rather a why-did-they-do-it, the very extremism of the communal deed creating considerable curiosity in the reader. In preparing to answer that historical question in a novel, Matthiessen searched for six years through books, magazines, and newspapers for clues. More significant, however, were the recollections about Watson and the event by his family and descendants and his neighbor's descendants. Matthiessen says that he talked to at least one representative of nearly every family mentioned in the book. The result is an imagined version of events that the author admits "is in no way 'historical,' since almost nothing here is history." On the other hand, he adds, "there is nothing that could *not* have happened," and his hope is that "this reimagined life contains much more of the *truth* of Mister Watson than the lurid and popularly accepted 'facts' of the Watson legend."[2]

"Truth," says Taylor Branch in *Parting the Waters,* "requires a maximum effort to see through the eyes of strangers, foreigners, and enemies."[3] As if impelled by this insight, Matthiessen tells the story of Watson through the first-person accounts of ten different speakers, all of whom reminisce about the man. Mister Watson is already dead, and the voices fade in and out as their recollections reconstruct events beginning with his first appearance in the Chokoloskee Bay area, the gateway to Florida's Ten Thousand Islands, a remote area frequented by drifters, renegades, and other outcasts from society. The speakers talk in a relative vacuum, answering only the implicit

question—What do you know about Mister Watson—and they appear and
return at irregular intervals, each chapter preceded by the lone heading of
the speaker's name. Narrative flow is accomplished by the frequent intervention of an "author's" starkly objective recapitulation of the actions. This
"author," himself a fiction, is an aspiring historian, whose careful amalgam
of events tries to balance the contradictory and mediate the probable, providing a plain précis of Watson's life. This account is in italics along with
occasional excerpts from contemporary newspaper columns, both of these
providing a continuous and somewhat objective strand to the discontinuous
and subjective recollections.

The multivoiced technique filters the reality of Watson through ten different minds, all with their own predispositions, situated at varying removes
from the man himself, who ultimately was not intimate with any of the
speakers and perhaps with no one at all. The most frequently appearing
voice and one that spans the greater part of the book belongs to Bill House,
one of the proud killers of Watson, whose family was a direct competitor to
Watson's farming and export business. Another House, Bill's sister Mamie,
speaks her critical mind about Watson as well, but Mamie's criticism is
tempered by her role as wife of Ted Smallwood, the town's Postmaster and
one of the few who opposed the killing. Matthiessen realizes that for truth
to emerge, it is necessary to hear from a man's friends as well as his enemies.
And while we do not hear directly from Ted Smallwood, his opinion about
Watson is a constant reference point of the book, indirectly culled by our
historian-narrator from a published account of his reminiscences. We also
hear from a man who worked for Watson longer than anyone and who defends him to the end, and from various members of the family that lived
closest to the Watson place. Even the sheriff who tried to take Watson into
custody and who interrogated his killers speaks his ambiguous piece. One
of the most frequent voices emerges from the diary of Watson's daughter
Carrie, whose entries delight in their affectionate simplicity and loyalty. The
many voices cast Mister Watson in different lights, illuminating the figure
more fully than any other means of telling could have done. By the book's
end, the enigma of Watson and his killing has not been eliminated, but it
has been viewed from so many different angles that it is no longer incomprehensible. We see a powerful, charming, dangerous, generous, and enormously enterprising man, a man as capable of uprooting his family to
another state as of leaving it and moving himself, as capable of helping out
a neighbor in need as of shooting a neighbor in his way, a man whose will is
synonymous with action.

In revealing Watson, the historical figure, Matthiessen's novel also exhibits the awesome complexity of historical events, how the true story of anyone's life is initially hidden but finally uncovered by conflicting interpretations. Mister Watson in the end is no longer a stranger obscured by legend. He is a man with both light and dark sides. As his wife Jane's note shows, it is this dark side that occasioned the trouble in his life and his eventual death. She tells her daughter: "There is a wound in your poor father I could never heal. . . . He is a man, a human being, whose violence is only the dark part of him, there is also a life-giving side that flourishes in the full light" (*KMW*, 370).

The voices work. They are interesting and their tones are different enough to establish individuality, while they are all cut from the general speech pattern of the area. Matthiessen has always had an ear for the way people talk, and it serves him splendidly here, sometimes to humorous effect, as when we hear one of the tellers, Henry Thompson, relate the end of one "thin, piney-woods cracker" who had shot an occasional neighbor:

> Will must have been wanted pretty bad—dead or alive, as you might say. Probably should have picked him a new name, got a fresh start, cause the law got wind of him some way and deputies come a-hunting him, out of Key West. Will said Nosir, he'd be damned if he'd go peaceable, and he whistled a bullet past their heads to prove it. But he was peaceable and then some by the time the smoke cleared, so they threw his carcass in the boat. The law asked the Widder Raymond would she and her daughter like a boat ride to Key West along with the deceased, and she said, Thankee, don't mind if we do. (*KMW*, 14–15)

This method of multiple narrators recalls Faulkner's experiments with voice, especially in *As I Lay Dying*. Other than Faulkner, I know of no novelist as successful as Matthiessen in building a society, a complete milieu, from a variety of first-person narrators. For, while Watson is the pole around which the separate narratives revolve, each tells hundreds of other stories: about the Calusa Indian burial grounds, about the runaway slaves who fought side by side with the Seminole Indians, about the hunters for bird plumes and gator hides, about the settlers who'd pull out the government's channel markers to discourage outsiders, about the farming and the selling and the Fort Meyers cattle business, about the saloons and the drinking and the shooting in a place where "men settled their differences amongst themselves, and a killing was not what you might call uncommon . . ." (*KMW*, 56). In *Far Tortuga*, as well, Matthiessen employed the pattern of letting the world of the novel emerge from voice, but the voices of the earlier novel were strictly limited to conversation. Here each speaker is given space and time to tell his or her own version of history. After all, initially and therefore crucially it is voice, individual voice, that transmits history and fact. Since any one voice is bound to be unbalanced by its unique personality and prejudices, however, what Matthiessen has done, and Faulkner before him, is to overlay voices, each with its own rich experience and interpretation of events, allowing patterns of corroboration, consensus, and doubt to emerge. This does not produce the certainty of third-person omniscient narration, but it does imitate the way historical events are reported and finally understood.

Eric Bentley advises the would-be dramatist in *The Life of the Drama*: "if you wish to attract the audience's attention, be violent; if you wish to hold it, be violent again."[4] Bentley goes on to say that a lot of bad plays are written following this advice, but no good ones are written defying it. The very dramatic *Killing Mister Watson* does not defy it. Not only does the novel have a violent incident at its center, but it is strewn with accounts of killings and confrontations in a lawless time and place in U.S. history. In attempting to imaginatively recreate the events leading up to Watson's demise, the novel becomes in the voices of its ten speakers a prolonged meditation on violence. There is, of course, the trail of bodies that seems to follow Watson wherever he goes, from South Carolina to Oklahoma to Arkansas to Florida. He may well have killed his own brother-in-law; he was arraigned for the murder of the legendary outlaw Belle Starr but released because of insufficient evidence; by his own admission, he dispatched the knife-wielding Quinn Bass; and it is rumored that he is wanted for murder in three states.

The final straw in a pile of accumulating suspicions about Watson's lawless violence is the murder of three of his workers followed by an eye-witness allegation, later withdrawn, that Watson himself had ordered his foreman to do the deed. Although the townsmen are never sure that Watson was behind the murders or was present when they occurred, they act upon a test of Watson's word. He promises to either return with the killer or bring back his head. When he fails to do either, claiming the foreman fell into the water when shot, the townsmen kill Watson. They base their action on no one crime of Watson. They simply feel that too much blood has been spilled by him and around him, and that the law has proved inadequate to respond, either because of Watson's prominent Fort Meyers political connections or because of his craftiness and boldness. Whatever the case, the men are effectively galvanized into action by the accumulation of horribles surrounding Watson. He may or may not have been guilty of this latest murder, but he is unquestionably a violent man who is menacing when crossed, and he refuses to be disarmed. Since they have no determinative evidence and feel there can be none, their decision hinges on the somewhat arbitrary point of Watson's failure to keep his word. They have drawn a line, and Watson has crossed it. That is enough.

One of the subthemes of the novel is the problematic nature of justice without a rigorous and firm system of law. When one of the townsmen tries to cajole Ted Smallwood into joining them by reminding him of Watson's cold-blooded killings, Ted replies, "Ain't nobody proved that in a court of law!" And the townsman fires back, "Ain't no law down here to prove it by" (*KMW*, 7). Because there is no such thing as local law enforcement, and desperados are allowed to use the Ten Thousand Islands as a haven, men are prone to balancing their own scales. In fact, what we have is an area that is formed by the very absence of law, trying to govern itself by rough and instinctive justice. So, Watson's fate is decided arbitrarily by the rough tally of corpses left in his wake, none of which is definitively linked to him by a line of hard evidence. In such circumstances, personal passion and self-interest obscure objective judgment about right and wrong, although the citizens preserve a sense of the difference between the two and a desire to do the right thing.

Even where the legal system is more vigorous, as in the cities like Fort Meyers, there are other obstacles to justice. Watson, it is almost universally believed, was acquitted for a murder in a northern county because of his highly placed connections, his son-in-law being the business partner of the politically influential Jim Cole. Sheriffs routinely abuse their authority even more blatantly and unfairly. Frank Tippins seems a sheriff of impeccable integrity, even to the point of risking his own life in the line of duty, but this same Tippins cares nothing about the apparent lynching of a black man who admitted he had been forced into firing into the dead body of a white woman. The sheriff feels the lynch mob saved the state the expense of a trial that would have convicted the black anyway. When law enforcement itself and the judicial system routinely cut corners in the administration of justice, it is no wonder that the justice of the street is rough and uneven.

Tippins's treatment of the black man not only shows the miscarriage of justice, but it also is an example of the other kinds of violence with which the book is concerned: the violence of men on women, that of the majority white race upon its Indian and black minorities, and even man's violence against his environment. Instances of these abound: wives abused by husbands, blacks cuffed or killed in punishment for supposed offenses, Indians pushed further back into the swamps or sent packing out west, entire rookeries of plume birds slaughtered with only the young chicks left in their undefended nests. Man does not bother replenishing the soil, and the whole system breaks down: "That black soil on the shell mounds had no minerals to speak of, just tuckered out in a few years, same as the women." For a time, with the land going sterile, the men turned to "bird plumes, gator hides, and pelts of coon and otter. Then the wild things give out, too," until "there wasn't much left to us but ricking buttonwood, a little fishing" (*KMW*, 202).

All of these instances of man's violence in the novel are reflected in the macrocosm of nature. Between the time of the murders down by Lost Man's River and the killing of Mister Watson, a major hurricane, the worst in memory, lashes the Florida coast. The hurricane of 1910 is as historical as Watson's death, so it is as if nature herself provided her own symbolism, one which Matthiessen uses in the novel: "In the hurricane's wake, the labyrinthine coast where the Everglades deltas meet the Gulf of Mexico lies broken, stunned, flattened to mud by the wild tread of God. Day after day, a gray and brooding wind nags at the mangroves, hurrying the unruly tides that hunt through the broken islands and twist far back into the creeks, leaving behind brown spume and matted salt grass, driftwood. On the bay shores and down the coastal rivers, a far gray sun picks up dead glints from windrows of rotted mullet, heaped a foot high" (*KMW*, 3). Nature itself lashes out after all the lashings of man. Violence begets violence, the rotted mullet redolent of the human carnage. The macrocosm reflects the microcosm.

Killing Mister Watson gathers together a number of the characteristic concerns of Matthiessen's other works. The black-white racial theme was present in his first and last short stories, and both of the other major novels also dealt with the question of mixed blood and the resulting prejudice. Injustice to Indians, more setting than theme in *Killing Mister Watson,* harkens back to the appearance of the Indian half-blood in his first novel, *Race Rock,* the emergence of a similar figure into the role of a major character in *At Play in the Fields of the Lord,* and, of course, Matthiessen's systematic attention to the plight of the American Indian in two works of nonfiction, *Indian Country* and *In the Spirit of Crazy Horse.* The question of man's violence upon his environment has always been a hallmark of Matthiessen's work, his nonfiction, of course, containing his most explicit indictments of the human ravages inflicted on the earth and its wild creatures, beginning with his first book in the genre, *Wildlife in America.*

Matthiessen's fascination with the historical E. J. Watson fits his life-long interest in the figure of the mysterious stranger, the taciturn outsider who lives a life of action, makes his own way, and stands up to whoever opposes him. The same figure, plus or minus a feature, appears throughout his fiction. He is Cady of *Race Rock*, Jacobi of *Partisans*, Lewis Meriwether Moon of *At Play in the Fields of the Lord*. The figure typically has had to deal with adversity, a determinative element in the formation of his character, which continues to be defined by an uneasy friction with society at large. Violence often occurs around this figure, even when he is not its direct perpetrator. Matthiessen's nonfiction, as well, features individuals cut in this mode. Leonard Peltier, Cesar Chavez, and the fishermen of South Fork are all strong men of action, at odds with society at large. And, in some sense, the collective manhood of the uncivilized tribes Matthiessen has visited around the world fits this mold in relation to civilized society, imaging the very otherness of nature at its wildest and most remote: silent, strong, and hostile.

When one looks at the centrality and influence of Matthiessen's family background, with one of his childhood residences on New York's Central Park, it does not take a genius to see his interest in the mysterious stranger as being a projection of everything he was not, at least not on the surface. We know that Matthiessen has never felt comfortable with the world of money and privilege to which he was born. I will not delve into speculative psychological analysis here, but perhaps the power of Matthiessen's writing in part derives from his ability to tap into his dark side, his Jungian shadow. If so, it would explain at least one similarity between him and the writers to whom he is sometimes compared in his major fiction: Melville, Conrad, and Dostoevsky.

Chapter Ten
Literary Perspective: Many Roles, One Birthright

Naturalist, novelist, explorer, advocate, and pilgrim, Peter Matthiessen has created an impressive body of work in his over forty-year literary career. He is perhaps best known for his nonfiction, especially for his evocations of the great and small spirits of the natural world; and the preponderance of his writing, over two-thirds of the books and a higher percentage of the magazine pieces, has been nonfiction. As a chronicler, Matthiessen characteristically writes of nature's least tamed places with elegant precision, blending a scientist's respect for fact with a contemplative's reverence for mystery. His greatest achievements in the genre, *The Snow Leopard, The Cloud Forest,* and *The Tree Where Man Was Born* discover correspondences between nature's riches and man's needs, each book embodying its discovery in a central and explanatory metaphor, thus creating a myth. This mythic dimension separates these books from the rest of Matthiessen's nonfiction, although two of his other books, *Men's Lives* and *Under the Mountain Wall,* are unique and fine in their own right. And in all of his nonfiction, Matthiessen is an informative guide and painstaking artist in words.

Matthiessen's most significant writing, however, is his fiction. *Far Tortuga* is not only one of the great sea novels, as has been argued by Bert Bender, but it is among the dozen or so novels in the last twenty-five years that have added distinctive contours to the landscape of American fiction. The book's originality derives from its total fusion of realism and lyricism. At a time when other novelists like Borges, Barth, and Coover were experimenting along the similar lines of magical realism—challenging the reader's traditional assumptions about narrative time, authorial detachment, and the inevitability of plausible narrative sequence—Matthiessen was experimenting with narrative technique in an entirely different manner, suppressing the authorial narrator altogether, expressing action by dialogue, and using a narrative voice so impersonal that it assumes the face of nature itself.

Imagine someone falling asleep after reading Dreiser's *Sister Carrie* in 1903 and awakening like Rip Van Winkle some years later (seventy-three in this case) to Matthiessen's *Far Tortuga.* The shock of form would be so terrific that the reader would doubtless not even call Matthiessen's book a novel. He would, in fact, lack language to describe the work. To see *Far Tortuga* thus casts light on how affected Matthiessen has been by the modernist technical innovations in the novel's form, especially Faulkner's experiments with voice, and Hemingway's and Fitzgerald's tightening of style. Matthiessen's technical experimentation in *Far Tortuga*, as well as in the recent *Killing Mister Watson,* are clearly built upon the foundations of modernism, which pushed formal and technical efforts to the fore.

Despite the huge formal chasm between Dreiser's and Matthiessen's novels, there is also a surprising similarity. The power of environment that is so determinative in Dreiser and the other naturalists, coursing through *Sister Carrie* as the quickened pulse of city life, remarkably resembles the combined power of nature and the modern world that drives the captain and crew of the *Lillias Eden* to their end in *Far Tortuga*. What Richard Poirier calls "the conglomerations [that] go under different names: Nature, The City, Society, The Dynamo"[1] are as central to Matthiessen's novel as they were to Dreiser's and to those of the other naturalists. Given his Darwinian view of the natural world as expressed in his nonfiction, it should come as no surprise that Matthiessen is a naturalist in more ways than one. In his two other major novels, the power of "the conglomerations" is manifest largely as the force of nature. It is the wilderness itself in *At Play in the Fields of the Lord,* seen as a great magnet drawing civilized man to its center. In *Killing Mister Watson,* the external power of nature expresses itself in the great hurricane of 1910, but this force is less essential to the novel's core, which involves a primarily human drama, than in either of the other two books.

Killing Mister Watson continues the experimentation with narrative technique begun by Matthiessen in *Far Tortuga,* while *At Play in the Fields of the Lord,* the earliest of the major novels, is the author's one venture into the thickly realistic, conventionally narrated mainstream novel. It also happens to be his most popular book to date, with over 700,000 total copies sold.[2] This trio of novels, along with the stories "On the River Styx" and "Lumumba Lives," represent the best of Matthiessen's work. They are his legacy to the future.

No other novelist of Matthiessen's stature (Bruce Chatwin and Paul Theroux are not) has spent as much time as he in other kinds of writing—perhaps too much, as he himself acknowledged in his preface to *On the River Styx and Other Stories.* Yet each of his books, each journey and each article, seems to have evolved from a philosophy that was Zen even before Matthiessen knew it. In *The Snow Leopard,* he wrote, "I am not here to seek the 'crazy wisdom'; if I am, I shall never find it. I am here to be here . . ."

(*SL*, 113). Each book has been a response to what it meant "to be here," although the particular "here" ranges from the cosmopolitan cities of New York and Paris to the remotest outposts of human habitation in New Guinea and Africa. Of course, Matthiessen was often under contract to the *New Yorker* to write an account of particular trips, such as his visits to Tanzania's Selous Game Reserve or the Peruvian wilderness. In most cases, whether the trip was underwritten or not, the nonfictional response seemed to exhaust the experience. There was no more to tell about the search for the great white shark or the labor organizing of Cesar Chavez. Occasionally, however, as with the South American journey and his adventure on an old schooner out of Grand Cayman, the factual account simply would not suffice, for the true experience was not what happened but what the author had imagined. In those cases, novels resulted.

Each of his books, then, has been a response to the unexpected Now, carefully attending to the insights of the moment. His books are based upon experience and research, usually direct experience. This is the common ground between his fiction and his nonfiction. Because fundamentally each book is a direct response to experience, its form as well as its content depends on the nature and shape of each experience. This explains the wide variety of roles and voices in his nonfiction, as well as the shifting between the two genres. His first books were novels; and, while nonfiction has subsequently dominated his writing, he has now returned to the novel like an heir to his birthright.

Matthiessen lives by turning to new tasks. He strikes me as a man who wastes no time on transitions, whether in everyday events around the house like raking the sludge from an old pond, having lunch, and returning to his study to write, or in major turnings in his life like going to Paris, founding the *Paris Review,* leaving Paris, and becoming a commercial fisherman. This characteristic undoubtedly is one of the secrets of his immense productivity. Now sixty-four years old and still vigorous in mind and body, he shows no signs of slowing down. There is no telling how much he has yet to write. Based on the quality of the recent *Killing Mister Watson,* his novelistic skills are as strong as ever. When I asked about his plans for future writing, he envisioned only one or two more nonfiction projects: the island book mentioned in chapter one and another book about Africa, to be called *African Silences,* both of them largely completed.[3] Otherwise, he plans to concentrate on fiction and is now at work on the second volume of his projected *Watson* trilogy. Matthiessen sees the novel as the form of his deepest inspirations and the role of novelist as his highest calling. Each of his works, however, is a moment in the journey, and according to his Zen beliefs, each moment is all.

Notes and References

Chapter One

1. Matthiessen has privately printed an essay on his lineage, primarily for his siblings and their children, called "Homegoing." It has no page numbers, no date, and no publisher's imprint.

2. This visit occurred on 13 January 1989. On a subsequent visit seven months later on August 10, Matthiessen and I would bike to the beach, lie upon the hot summer sand, and talk into a tape recorder that I failed to turn on correctly.

3. Peter Matthiessen, *Men's Lives* (New York: Random House, 1986; New York: Vintage, 1988), 102; hereafter cited in text as *ML*.

4. Peter Matthiessen, "New York: Old Hometown," *Architectural Digest,* November 1989, 66,70; hereafter cited in text as "NY."

5. John Wakeman, ed., *World Authors: 1950–70* (New York: H. W. Wilson, 1975), 956; hereafter cited in text as *World Authors*.

6. Peter Matthiessen, *The Snow Leopard* (New York: Viking, 1978; New York: Penguin, 1987), 42–43; hereafter cited in text as *SL*.

7. Gay Talese, "Looking for Hemingway," *Esquire,* July 1963, 106; hereafter cited in the text.

8. William Styron, *This Quiet Dust* (New York: Random House, 1982), 249; hereafter cited in the text.

9. Janet Flanner, *Paris Journal 1945–1955* (New York: Harvest, 1965), 189.

10. William Styron, "Letter to an Editor," *Paris Review,* February 1953, 10–11.

11. Malcolm Cowley, *Exile's Return* (New York: Viking, 1951; New York: Penguin, 1976), 6; hereafter cited in the text.

12. Wendy Smith, "PW Interviews Peter Matthiessen," *Publishers Weekly,* 9 May 1986, 241; hereafter cited in the text.

13. Personal interview, Sagaponack, N.Y., 10 August 1989.

14. Peter Matthiessen, *Nine-Headed Dragon River* (Boston: Shambhala, 1985), 5; hereafter cited in text as *NHDR*.

Chapter Two

1. Quoted in Michael Shnayerson, *Irwin Shaw: a Biography* (New York: Putnam's, 1989), 205–6; hereafter cited in the text.

2. Styron quotes these very words from Malcolm Cowley's *The Second Flowering* in his 1973 review, which is reprinted in *This Quiet Dust,* 92.

3. Peter Matthiessen, *Race Rock* (New York: Harper & Bros., 1954; Vintage, 1988), 35–36; hereafter cited in the text as *RR*.

4. Peter Matthiessen, *Partisans* (New York: Viking, 1955; Vintage, 1987), 30; hereafter cited in the text as *P*.

5. Peter Matthiessen, *Raditzer* (New York: Viking, 1961; Vintage, 1987), 40; hereafter cited in the text as *R*.

6. Maurice Cranston, *London Magazine,* 2 June 1955, 101. Cranston got Matthiessen's age wrong, calling him thirty-three when he was, in fact, twenty-eight.

7. William Goyen, *New York Times Book Review,* 2 October 1955, 4.

8. James Finn, *Commonweal,* 28 October 1955, 103.

9. Granville Hicks, *Saturday Review,* 28 January 1961, 14.

10. *New Yorker,* 22 April 1961, 178–79.

Chapter Three

1. Ralph Waldo Emerson, "Self-Reliance," *The Essays of Ralph Waldo Emerson* (New York: Random House, 1944), 39; hereafter cited in the text.

2. Ralph Waldo Emerson, "The Poet," *The Essays of Ralph Waldo Emerson* (New York: Random House, 1944), 222; hereafter cited in the text.

3. See Emerson's discussion of the topic in "Nature," *The Essays of Ralph Waldo Emerson* (New York: Random House, 1944), 319 ff.

4. Peter Matthiessen, *Wildlife in America* (New York: Viking, 1959; 1987), 141; hereafter cited in the text as *WA*.

5. Both trips resulted in articles: "Among The Griz," *Outside*, September 1990; and "The Blue Pearl of Siberia," *New York Review of Books*, 14 February 1991.

6. Francis Parkman, *The Oregon Trail* (New York: Dodd, Mead, 1964), xiii.

7. Edward Weeks, *Atlantic,* March 1960, 110–11.

8. Rae Brooks, *Harper's Magazine,* November 1959, 118.

9. Archie Carr, "The Need to Let Live," *New York Times Book Review,* 22 November 1959, 38.

10. *Wilderness,* Spring 1988, 68.

11. Peter Matthiessen, *The Shorebirds of North America*, ed. Gardner D. Stout (New York: Viking, 1967), 115.

12. Walter Harding, *Library Journal* 92 (1967):4168.

13. John Hay, *Natural History,* January 1968, 70.

14. R. M. Mengel, *Book World,* 10 December 1967, 5.

15. Peter Farb, *Saturday Review,* 25 November 1967, 44.

16. Peter Matthiessen, *The Wind Birds* (New York: Viking, 1973), 16. Subsequent quotes are from this edition and will be cited in the text as *WB*.

17. Wallace Stevens, *The Collected Poems of Wallace Stevens* (New York:

Knopf, 1954) 70, 92. The first reference is to "Sunday Morning"; the second to "Peter Quince at the Clavier."

Chapter Four

1. Peter Nabokov, "Return to the Native," *New York Review of Books,* 27 September 1984, 45.

2. Ronald Weber, *The Literature of Fact: Literary Nonfiction in American Writing* (Athens, Ohio: Ohio University Press, 1980), 2.

3. John Hollowell, *Fact & Fiction: The New Journalism and the Nonfiction Novel* (Chapel Hill: North Carolina University Press, 1986), 11.

4. Peter Matthiessen, *The Cloud Forest: A Chronicle of the South American Wilderness* (New York: Viking, 1961; New York: Penguin, 1987), 63; hereafter cited in the text as *CF.*

5. "The Subtle Explorer," *Newsweek,* 9 October 1961, 105.

6. W. Ross Winterowd discusses the literary qualities of *The Snow Leopard* in his *The Rhetoric of the "Other" Literature* (Carbondale: Southern Illinois University Press, 1990) 133–39.

7. Milan Kundera, *The Art of the Novel* (New York: Grove, 1988), 31, 142.

8. Provided, of course, the experiences do not remain so personally threatening that dealing factually with them is unbearable. In that case, a fiction of the experience might be used as a buffer.

Chapter Five

1. Terrence Des Pres, "Soul Searching in the Himalayas," Review of *The Snow Leopard, Washington Post,* 20 August 1970, E1; hereafter cited in the text.

2. Ralph Waldo Emerson, "Nature," *The Essays of Ralph Waldo Emerson* (New York: Random, 1944), 329.

3. Rudolf Otto, *The Idea of the Holy,* trans. John W. Harvey (New York: Oxford, 1923; 1958), 26.

4. Peter Matthiessen, *Under the Mountain Wall: A Chronicle of Two Seasons in Stone Age New Guinea* (New York: Viking, 1962; New York: Penguin, 1987), xiii; hereafter cited in the text as *UMW.*

5. Peter Matthiessen, *Oomingmak: The Expedition to the Musk Ox Island in the Bering Sea* (New York: Hastings House, 1967), 11; hereafter cited in the text as *O.*

6. Peter Matthiessen, *Blue Meridian* (New York: Random House, 1971), 83; hereafter cited in the text as *BM.*

7. Peter Matthiessen, *The Tree Where Man Was Born* (New York: Dutton, 1972; 1983), 273; hereafter cited in the text as *TWMB.*

8. Peter Matthiessen, *Sand Rivers* (New York: Viking, 1981), 3; hereafter cited in the text as *SR.*

Chapter Six

1. Ralph Waldo Emerson, "Experience," *The Essays of Ralph Waldo Emerson* (New York: Random, 1944), 254.
2. Henry David Thoreau, *Walden and Civil Disobedience,* ed. Owen Thomas (New York: Norton, 1966), 218.
3. Walt Whitman, "Song of Myself," *Leaves of Grass* (Philadelphia: David McKay, 1891–92; New York: Bantam, 1983), 32.
4. Peter Matthiessen, *Sal Si Puedes: Cesar Chavez and the New American Revolution* (New York: Random House, 1969), 177; hereafter cited in the text as *SSP.*
5. Martin Garbus [Matthiessen's and Viking's attorney in the libel action], "The F.B.I. Man Who Cried Libel," *The Nation,* 13 November 1989, 564.
6. U.S. Court of Appeals for the Eighth Circuit, "David Price, Appellant, v. Viking Penguin, Inc. and Peter Matthiessen Appellees," No. 88–5075, 1989, U.S. App. Lexis 11441, 25.
7. Peter Matthiessen, *In the Spirit of Crazy Horse* (New York: Viking, 1983), 29; hereafter cited in the text as *SCH.*
8. Unfortunately, forensic evidence does not reveal all the circumstances of an action. Matthiessen reports that he recently has heard firsthand testimony that the killing of Agent Williams was done in self-defense. Let us hope this new evidence will clarify the killings in the revised version of *Crazy Horse,* which is scheduled to appear in 1991.
9. Peter Matthiessen, *Indian Country* (New York: Viking, 1984), 74; hereafter cited in the text as *IC.*
10. Peter Nabokov, "Return to the Native," *New York Review of Books,* 27 September 1984, 45; hereafter cited in the text.

Chapter Seven

1. Peter Matthiessen, "To the Miskito Bank," *New Yorker,* 28 October 1967, 146; hereafter cited in the text as "Miskito."
2. "Editors' Choice: 1975," *New York Times Book Review,* 24 December 1975, 2.
    Robert Stone, *New York Times Book Review,* 25 May 1975, 1.
    Edward Weeks, *Atlantic Monthly,* June 1975, 92.
    Booklist, 15 July 1975, 1162.
    William Kennedy, *New Republic,* 7 June 1975, 28, 30.
    Dave Smith, *Library Journal,* 15 April 1975, 783.
    Peter S. Prescott, *Newsweek,* 19 May 1975, 86.
    Anatole Broyard, *New York Times,* 6 May 1975, 37.
    Publisher's Weekly, 1 March 1975, 50.
3. Peter Matthiessen, "The Craft of Fiction in *Far Tortuga,*" interview by

George Plimpton, *Paris Review*, Winter 1974, 81; hereafter cited in the text as "Craft."

    4. Peter Matthiessen, *Far Tortuga* (New York: Random House, 1975), 354; hereafter cited in the text as *FT*.

    5. Thomas Edwards, "Adventures of the Deep," *New York Review of Books*, 7 August 1975, 35.

    6. Paul Gray, "Sea Changes," *Time*, 26 May 1975, 80.

    7. See James Grove, "Pastoralism and Anti-Pastoralism in Peter Matthiessen's *Far Tortuga*," *Critique* 21:2 (1979):15–29; hereafter cited in the text. Grove interprets the Captain's railings at the modern world as a consequence of his longing for the pastoral ideal. He says, "In Raib's quest for Far Tortuga, Matthiessen depicts an àttempted pastoral escape doomed from the start" (23). Grove's article is excellent in its attention to the novel's details, and his explanation parallels, in a more elaborate fashion, my comments on the contrast between old and new ways. Despite "pastoralism's" ability, especially in the broad understanding of the term by William Empson, to accommodate Raib's vision, I am not comfortable with its use in this context. Raib's is essentially a sea vision of a place where green turtles abound, by a man who makes his living catching turtles.

    8. Bert Bender, "*Far Tortuga* and American Sea Fiction Since *Moby-Dick*," *American Literature* 56:2 (1984):237. Although in my view *Far Tortuga* has not received nearly the critical attention it deserves, what it has received has been of high quality. Bender's fine article places the novel in the context of other sea stories, concluding: "Like the greatest works of art in any tradition, *Far Tortuga* feeds on and yet renews its heritage, the still vital tradition of American sea fiction. In its constant sensitivity to all elements of the seascape—the light and dark, sun and stars, the green and often wind-whitened water; and especially in its sensitivity to the teeming life in, on, and above the water—it is more purely a *sea* novel than any in our literature" (247–48).

Chapter Eight

    1. In each of Matthiessen's books at least one observation of birds is made.

    2. Edward Hoagland, "Walking the Himalayas," *New York Times Book Review*, 13 August 1978, 1, 20–21.

    3. Jim Harrison, "Ten Thousand Octobers," *Nation*, 16 September 1978, 251.

    4. George Schaller, *Stones of Silence: Journeys in the Himalaya* (New York: Viking, 1980). Schaller's book makes interesting reading in its own right, as well as in contrast to Matthiessen's. There is a mixture of the scientific and the spiritual in both narratives, but the proportions are dramatically reversed. The two men, by their own accounts, shared little internally during the trek, recognizing and respecting each other's different purposes. Matthiessen departed the Crystal Mountain before Schaller, who found his companion's "frequent talk of leaving" a disquieting intrusion of "the future . . . on the present" (251–52) [an observation that has

ironic overtones in the context of Matthiessen's principal insights on the journey].
Schaller's book also contains photographs of the expedition party, including one of
the Lama of Shey.

5. C. G. Jung, *Collected Works* (Princeton, N.J.: Bollingen Foundation, for
the Princeton University Press, 1954); 17, chap. 7.

Chapter Nine

1. Peter Matthiessen, *On the River Styx and Other Stories* (New York: Random House, 1989), x; hereafter cited in the text as *ORS*.

2. Peter Matthiessen, *Killing Mister Watson* (New York: Random House,
1990), Author's Note; hereafter cited in the text as *KMW*.

3. Taylor Branch, *Parting the Waters: America in the King Years 1954–63*
(New York: Simon & Schuster, 1988), xii.

4. Eric Bentley, *The Life of the Drama* (New York: Atheneum, 1964), 9.

Chapter Ten

1. Richard Poirier, *A World Elsewhere: The Place of Style in American Literature* (New York: Oxford University Press, 1966), 237.

2. Rebecca Saletan, editor at Random House, personal telephone interview,
5 February 1990.

3. Peter Matthiessen, *African Silences* (New York: Random House, 1991).

Selected Bibliography

PRIMARY WORKS

Novels

At Play in the Fields of the Lord. New York: Random House, 1965.
_____. London: Heinemann, 1966.
_____. New York: New American Library, 1967.
_____. London: Panther, 1968.
_____. New York: Bantam, 1976.
_____. London: Granada, 1980.
_____. New York: Vintage, 1987.
_____. London: Collins Harvill, 1988.
Far Tortuga. New York: Random House, 1975.
_____. New York: Bantam, 1976.
_____. New York: Vintage, 1984.
_____. New York: Vintage, 1988.
_____. London: Collins Harvill, 1989.
Killing Mister Watson. New York: Random House, 1990.
_____. London: Collins Harvill, 1990.
Partisans. New York: Viking, 1955.
_____. New York: Avon Publications, 1955 (retitled: *The Passionate Seekers*).
_____. London: Secker & Warburg, 1956.
_____. London: Heinemann, 1966.
_____. New York: Vintage, 1987.
_____. London: Collins Harvill, 1990.
Race Rock. New York: Harper & Brothers, 1954.
_____. London: Secker & Warburg, 1954.
_____. New York: Bantam, 1957 [retitled *The Year of the Tempest*].
_____. London: Heinemann, 1966.
_____. New York: Vintage, 1988.
Raditzer. New York: Viking, 1961.
_____. London: Heinemann, 1961.
_____. New York: Dell, 1965.
_____. New York: Vintage, 1987.

Short Story Collections

Midnight Turning Gray. Bristol, R.I.: Ampersand Press, 1984.

On the River Styx and Other Stories. New York: Random House, 1989. Includes all
the stories from *Midnight Turning Gray,* plus two others.
_____. London: Collins Harvill, 1989.
_____. New York: Vintage, 1990.

Nonfiction

African Silences. New York: Random House, 1991.
Blue Meridian: The Search for the Great White Shark. New York: Random House,
1971.
_____. New York: New American Library, 1971.
The Cloud Forest: A Chronicle of the South American Wilderness. New York: Viking
Press, 1961.
_____. London: Andre Deutsch, 1962.
_____. New York: Ballantine, 1963.
_____. New York: Pyramid, 1966.
_____. New York: Penguin, 1987.
_____. London: Collins Harvill, 1988.
In the Spirit of Crazy Horse. New York: Viking, 1983.
Indian Country. New York: Viking, 1984.
_____. New York: Penguin, 1984.
_____. London: Collins Harvill, 1985.
_____. London: Flamingo, 1986.
Men's Lives. New York: Random House, 1986.
_____. New York: Rock Foundation, 1986.
_____. New York: Vintage, 1988.
_____. London: Collins Harvill, 1988.
Nine-Headed Dragon River: Zen Journals 1969–1982. Boston: Shambhala Publi-
cations, 1985.
_____. London: Collins Harvill, 1986.
Oomingmak: The Expedition to the Musk Ox Island in the Bering Sea. New York:
Hastings House, 1967.
Sal Si Puedes: Cesar Chavez and the New American Revolution. New York: Random
House, 1969.
_____. New York: Dell-Delta, 1969.
_____. Rev. ed. New York: Random House, 1973.
_____. New York: Dell-Laurel, 1973.
Sand Rivers. New York: Viking, 1981.
_____. London: Aurum, 1981.
_____. New York: Bantam, 1982.
Seal Pool. Garden City, N.Y.: Doubleday, 1972.
_____. London: Angus & Robertson, 1974 [retitled *The Great Auk Escape*].
The Snow Leopard. New York: Viking, 1978.
_____. New York: Viking, Literary Guild Book Club edition, 1978.

————. Franklin Center, Penn.: Franklin Library, 1978.

————. New York: Bantam, 1979.

————. London: Pan, 1980.

————. New York: Penguin, 1987.

————. London: Collins Harvill, 1989.

The Tree Where Man Was Born. New York: E. P. Dutton, 1972.

————. London: Collins, 1972.

————. New York: Crescent, 1972.

————. New York: Avon, 1974.

————. New York: Dutton Obelisk, 1983.

————. London: Picador, 1984.

Under the Mountain Wall: A Chronicle of Two Seasons in the Stone Age. New York: Viking, 1962.

————. London: Heinemann, 1963.

————. New York: Ballantine, 1969.

————. New York: Ballantine, 1972.

————. New York: Penguin, 1987 [henceforth retitled *Under the Mountain Wall: A Chronicle of Two Seasons in Stone Age New Guinea*].

————. London: Collins Harvill, 1989.

Wildlife in America. New York: Viking, 1959.

————. London: Andre Deutsch, 1960.

————. New York: Viking Compass, 1964.

————. New York: Penguin, 1977.

————. Rev., updated ed. New York: Viking, 1987.

The Wind Birds. New York: Viking, 1973 (The text of this book originally appeared in *The Shorebirds of North America,* ed. Gardner D. Stout, New York: Viking Press, 1967).

Edited Works

North American Indians by George Catlin. New York: Viking, 1989 [with introduction by Matthiessen].

Unpublished Material

Homegoing. Privately printed. An account of the author's trip to the Isle of Föhr in search of ancestral paternal history, including an account of the first Matthiessens in America.

Contributions to Books

"The Art of Fiction V: William Styron." In *Writers at Work: The Paris Review Interviews,* edited by Malcolm Cowley, 268–82. New York: Viking, 1958. Interview is by Matthiessen and George Plimpton.

"The Atlantic Coast." In *The American Heritage Book of Natural Wonders,* edited by Alvin M. Josephy, 9–48. New York: American Heritage, 1972.

"Common Miracles." In *Search,* edited by Jean Sulzberger, 25–30. New York: Harper & Row, 1979.

"Foreword" to *The Way of the White Clouds: A Buddhist Pilgrim in Tibet,* by Lama Anagarika Govinda. Boston: Shambhala Publications, 1988.

"Foreword" to *To Forget The Self: An Illustrated Guide to Zen Meditation,* by John D. Buksbazen. Los Angeles: Zen Center, 1977.

"Homegoing." In *The Children of Bladensfield,* by Evelyn D. Ward, 116–41. New York: Viking, 1978. An account of maternal family history and of the author's visit to Bladensfield, the ancestral home.

"In the Dragon Islands." In *The Audubon Wildlife Treasury,* edited by Les Line, 25–44. Philadelphia: Lippincott, 1976.

1000 Adventures: With Tales of Discovery, by Peter Matthiessen, et al. New York: Harmony Books, 1983.

"Search for the White Death." In *Men of Courage,* edited by William Robert Parker, 163–76. Chicago: Playboy Press, 1972.

"Selections from the writing of Peter Matthiessen." In *Everglades,* by Patricia Caulfield. San Francisco: Sierra Club, 1970.

SECONDARY WORKS

Interviews

Allen, Henry. "Quest for the Snow Leopard's Secret: And Other Journeys Into Meaning with Best-Selling Author Peter Matthiessen." *The Washington Post,* 13 December 1978: D1, 15.

Bonetti, Kay. "An Interview with Peter Matthiessen." *The Missouri Review* 12, no. 2 (1989): 109–24.

Plimpton, George. "The Craft of Fiction in *Far Tortuga.*" *Paris Review* 15 (Winter 1974): 79–82.

Rea, Paul. "Causes and Creativity: An Interview with Peter Matthiessen." *Re Arts & Letters: A Liberal Arts Forum* 15 (Fall 1989): 27–40.

Smith, Wendy. "PW Interviews Peter Matthiessen." *Publishers Weekly,* 9 May 1986, 240–41.

Biographies

Cobbs, John L. "Peter Matthiessen." *American Novelists Since World War II: Second Series.* Vol. 6, *Dictionary of Literary Biography,* edited by James E. Kibler, Jr., 218–23. Detroit: Gale Research Co., 1980.

Dawidoff, Nicholas. "Earthbound in the Space Age: Peter Matthiessen Explores the Wild and the Majestic," *Sports Illustrated,* 3 December 1990, 119–24.

Gabriel, Trip. "The Nature of Peter Matthiessen." *New York Times Magazine*, 10 June 1990.

Love, Deborah. *Annaghkeen*. New York: Random House, 1970. An account by Matthiessen's second wife of the couple's trip to Ireland with their children Luke and Rue.

"Peter Matthiessen." *Current Biography*, 1975, 267–69.

"Peter Matthiessen." *World Authors 1950–1970*, edited by John Wakeman, 956–58. New York: H. W. Wilson Co., 1975.

Shnayerson, Michael. *Irwin Shaw*. New York: Putnam's, 1989. Scattered information about Matthiessen in Paris in the early 1950s.

Styron, William. "Peter Matthiessen," *This Quiet Dust and Other Writings*. New York: Random House, 1982: 249–52.

————. "The *Paris Review*," *This Quiet Dust and Other Writings*. New York: H. W. Wilson Co., 1975, 295–98.

Critical Studies

Bawer, Bruce. "Nature Boy: The Novels of Peter Matthiessen." *New Criterion* 6 (June 1988): 32–40. This is the only harsh assessment of Matthiessen's fiction. Although he pays lip service to the artistic achievement of *At Play in the Fields of the Lord* and *Far Tortuga,* Bawer reads both books as tracts against Western civilization, advocating a return to the wild. The reading, I believe, is wrong. Matthiessen is not anticulture; and, although he admires much about primitive peoples, he describes the hardships and aberrations of their lifestyles realistically.

Bender, Bert. "*Far Tortuga* and American Sea Fiction since *Moby-Dick*." *American Literature* 56 (May 1984): 227–48. An excellent article that places *Far Tortuga* just below *Moby-Dick* in the tradition of American sea fiction. Bender sees the vision and form of Matthiessen's novel as being shaped by "the sea's raw power." Matthiessen's independence, reliance on experience, Darwinism, and sense of wonder are illuminated in this context. Bender's attention to the novel's details in the light of other sea literature shows how great a work of art it is.

————. *Sea-Brothers: The Tradition of American Sea Fiction from Moby-Dick to the Present*. Philadelphia: University of Pennsylvania Press, 1988. Chapters 11 & 12 deal with Matthiessen. Chapter 12 is substantially the article from *American Literature*. Chapter 11 summarizes Matthiessen's briny experiences and discusses the sea context of other Matthiessen works, specifically *Race Rock, Raditzer,* and "Horse Latitudes," each of which, Bender argues, derives its central meaning from the sea.

Grove, James P. "Pastoralism and Anti-Pastoralism in Peter Matthiessen's *Far Tortuga*." *Critique* 21, no. 2 (1979): 15–29. Grove interprets the central conflict of the novel as between two visions: one longing for the good old days, the other living for today. He sees Matthiessen synthesizing the two opposing views in the figure of Speedy, who both lives in the here and now and retains the pastoral dream. Grove's analysis is perceptive, although his "pastoral/anti-pastoral" terminology seems more applied than organic.

Heim, Michael. "The Mystic and the Myth: Thoughts on *The Snow Leopard*." *Studia Mystica* 4 (Summer 1981): 3–9. Heim reads *The Snow Leopard* as a myth about the quest for mystical experience. Matthiessen, he suggests, does the impossible in conveying this myth through the linear form of a journal, for mystical experience is nonlinear and ineffable. It is only by subverting the linear pattern through the discovery of the sherpa Tutken's centrality and by suppressing any direct discussion of the mystical experience, as imaged by the snow leopard, that Matthiessen succeeds.

Patteson, Richard F. "*At Play in the Fields of the Lord*: The Imperialist Idea and the Discovery of the Self." *Critique* 21, no. 2 (1979): 5–14. Patteson insightfully sees the novel as using the trappings of the late 19th-century adventure literature ("the imperialist romance") to explore characteristically American themes like the flight from civilization and the discovery of self. Matthiessen, he argues, undercuts the old imperialist assumptions of superiority without advocating that "primal innocence is to be found in the woods" (13). Lewis Moon's final realization of his wild and civilized nature provides the novel's synthesis.

————. "Holistic Vision and Fictional Form in Peter Matthiessen's *Far Tortuga*." *Bulletin of the Rocky Mountain Modern Language Association* 37, no. 1–2 (1983): 70–81. This article points out the influence of Eastern thought and art on the form of *Far Tortuga*, which reflects a vision increasingly accepted by Western consciousness since the mid-1960s, namely that man is a small part of an interconnected universe, to which he must attune himself rather than vice versa. In his interpretation of the novel's resolution, Patteson, like Grove, sees Speedy as a normative character, not—as Grove would say—by holding onto the old pastoral dream while adapting to the present, but rather by discovering the dream through living in the present. This is another fine article that only adds to the novel's stature.

Winterowd, W. Ross. "Peter Matthiessen's Lyric Trek." In *The Rhetoric of the "Other" Literature*, 133–39. Carbondale, Ill.: Southern Illinois University Press, 1990. Winterowd uses *The Snow Leopard* as the climactic example of his thesis that nonfiction is capable of achieving a dimension every bit as "literary" as fiction. He exhibits the lyric and the thematic levels of Matthiessen's book, calling it "a magnificent achievement, having all the power of a great novel . . ." (133).

Bibliographies

Nicholas, D. *Peter Matthiessen: A Bibliography: 1951–1979.* Canoga Park, Calif.: Orirana Press, 1979. Primary and secondary, annotated. This indispensable tool lists book reviews and provides some biographical material as well.

Young, James Dean. "A Peter Matthiessen Checklist." *Critique* 21, no. 2 (1979): 30–38. Most items appear in Nicholas, but this checklist does add a few editions of Matthiessen's books and some secondary material not in the larger bibliography.

Index

The Author

William J. Dowie, Jr., grew up in New Orleans's Irish Channel. Educated by the Jesuits in high school and college, he went on to graduate school in English at Brandeis University on a Woodrow Wilson Fellowship, receiving the Ph.D. in 1970. He currently teaches at Southeastern Louisiana University, where he is Professor of English and Director of Graduate Studies in English.

Dr. Dowie's essays on modern literature have been published in *Novel: A Forum on Fiction, The Heythrop Journal, College English, Louisiana Literature,* and *Aethlon: The Journal of Sport Literature.* He has contributed articles on Walker Percy to *The Art of Walker Percy,* edited by Panthea Broughton (LSU Press, 1979), and *Critical Essays on Walker Percy* edited by J. Donald Crowley and Sue M. Crowley (G. K. Hall, 1989), and a piece on James Salter to *Essays on the Literature of Mountaineering,* edited by Armand Singer (West Virginia University Press, 1981). He has written occasional reviews on contemporary fiction for *America* magazine.

The Editor

Frank Day is a professor of English at Clemson University. He is the author of *Sir William Empson: An Annotated Bibliography* and *Arthur Koestler: A Guide to Research*. He was a Fulbright Lecturer in American Literature in Romania (1980–81) and in Bangladesh (1986–87).